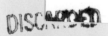

THE CONSTANT WIFE

KATHARINE CORNELL

THE
CONSTANT WIFE

A Comedy in Three Acts

BY

W. SOMERSET MAUGHAM

Garden City, New York

DOUBLEDAY & COMPANY, INC.

To
ETHEL BARRYMORE

THE CONSTANT WIFE *by W. Somerset Maugham was produced by Katharine Cornell at the National Theatre, New York City, on the night of December 9, 1951, with the following cast:*

(*In Order of Appearance*)

MRS. CULVER	Grace George
BENTLEY	Liam Sullivan
MARTHA CULVER	Gertrude Musgrove
BARBARA FAWCETT	Eva Leonard-Boyne
CONSTANCE MIDDLETON	Katharine Cornell
MARIE-LOUISE DURHAM	Nan Martin
JOHN MIDDLETON, F.R.C.S.	Brian Aherne
BERNARD KERSAL	John Emery
MORTIMER DURHAM	Claude Horton

THE CONSTANT WIFE

A Comedy in Three Acts

*The action of the play takes place in John's
house in Harley Street*

ACT ONE

SCENE: CONSTANCE'S *drawing room. It is a room furnished
with singularly good taste.* CONSTANCE *has a gift for
decoration and has made this room of hers both beautiful
and comfortable.*

It is afternoon.

MRS. CULVER *is seated alone. She is an elderly lady with
a pleasant face and she is dressed in walking costume. The
door is opened and* BENTLEY *the butler introduces* MARTHA
CULVER. *This is her daughter and a fine young woman.*

BENTLEY: Miss Culver.

[*He goes out.*]

MARTHA [*With astonishment*]: Mother.

MRS. CULVER [*Very calmly*]: Yes, darling.

MARTHA: You're the last person I expected to find here. You never told me you were coming to see Constance.

MRS. CULVER [*Good humouredly*]: I didn't intend to till I saw in your beady eye that *you* meant to. I thought I'd just as soon be here first.

MARTHA: Bentley says she's out.

MRS. CULVER: Yes. . . . Are you going to wait?

MARTHA: Certainly.

MRS. CULVER: Then I will too.

MARTHA: That'll be very nice.

MRS. CULVER: Your words are cordial, but your tone is slightly frigid, my dear.

MARTHA: I don't know what you mean by that, mother.

MRS. CULVER: My dear, we've known one another a great many years, haven't we? More than we always find it convenient to mention.

MARTHA: Not at all. I'm thirty-two. I'm not in the least ashamed of my age. Constance is thirty-six.

MRS. CULVER: And yet we still think it worth while to be a trifle disingenuous with one another. Our sex takes a natural pleasure in dissimulation.

MARTHA: I don't think any one can accuse me of not being frank.

MRS. CULVER: Frankness of course is the pose of the moment. It is often a very effective screen for one's thoughts.

MARTHA: I think you're being faintly disagreeable to me, mother.

MRS. CULVER: I, on the other hand, think you're inclined to be decidedly foolish.

MARTHA: Because I want to tell Constance something she ought to know?

MRS. CULVER: Ah, I *was* right then. And it's to tell her that you've broken an engagement, and left three wretched people to play cutthroat.

MARTHA: It is.

MRS. CULVER: And may I ask why you think Constance ought to know?

MARTHA: Why? Why? Why? That's one of those questions that really don't need answering.

MRS. CULVER: I've always noticed that the questions that really don't need answering are the most difficult to answer.

MARTHA: It isn't at all difficult to answer. She ought to know the truth becaues it's the truth.

MRS. CULVER: Of course truth is an excellent thing, but before one tells it one should be quite sure that one does so for the advantage of the person who hears it rather than for one's own self-satisfaction.

MARTHA: Mother, Constance is a very unhappy person.

MRS. CULVER: Nonsense. She eats well, sleeps well, dresses well and she's losing weight. No woman can be unhappy in those circumstances.

MARTHA: Of course if you won't understand it's no use my trying to make you. You're a darling, but you're the most unnatural mother. Your attitude simply amazes me.

[*The door opens and* BENTLEY *ushers in* MRS. FAWCETT. MRS. FAWCETT *is a trim, business-like woman of forty.*]

BENTLEY: Mrs. Fawcett.

MRS. CULVER: Oh, Barbara, how very nice to see you.

BARBARA [*Going up to her and kissing her*]: Bentley told me you were here and Constance was out. What are you doing?

MRS. CULVER: Bickering.

BARBARA: What about?

MRS. CULVER: Constance.

MARTHA: I'm glad you've come, Barbara. . . . Did you know that John was having an affair with Marie-Louise?

BARBARA: I hate giving a straight answer to a straight question.

MARTHA: I suppose every one knows but us. How long have you known? They say it's been going on for months. I can't think how it is we've only just heard it.

MRS. CULVER [*Ironically*]: It speaks very well for human nature that with the masses of dear friends we have it's only to-day that one of them broke the news to us.

BARBARA: Perhaps the dear friend only heard it this morning.

MARTHA: At first I refused to believe it.

MRS. CULVER: Only quite, quite at first, darling. You surrendered to the evidence with an outraged alacrity that took my breath away.

MARTHA: Of course I put two and two together. After the first shock I understood everything. I'm only astonished that it never occurred to me before.

BARBARA: Are you very much upset, Mrs. Culver?

MRS. CULVER: Not a bit. I was brought up by a very strict mother to believe that men were naturally wicked. I am seldom surprised at what they do and never upset.

MARTHA: Mother has been simply maddening. She treats it as though it didn't matter a row of pins.

MRS. CULVER: Constance and John have been married for fifteen years. John is a very agreeable man. I've sometimes wondered whether he was any more faithful to his wife than most husbands, but as it was really no concern of mine I didn't let my mind dwell on it.

MARTHA: Is Constance your daughter or is she not your daughter?

MRS. CULVER: You certainly have a passion for straight questions, my dear. The answer is yes.

MARTHA: And are you prepared to sit there quietly and let her husband grossly deceive her with her most intimate friend?

MRS. CULVER: So long as she doesn't know I can't see that she's any the worse. Marie-Louise is a nice little thing, silly of course, but that's what men like, and if John is going to deceive Constance it's much better that it should be with some one we all know.

MARTHA [*To* BARBARA]: Did you ever hear a respectable woman—and mother is respectable. . . .

MRS. CULVER [*Interrupting*]: Oh, quite.

MARTHA: Talk like that?

BARBARA: You think that something ought to be done about it?

MARTHA: I am determined that something shall be done about it.

MRS. CULVER: Well, my dear, I'm determined that there's at least one thing you shan't do and that is to tell Constance.

BARBARA [*A trifle startled*] : Is that what you want to do?

MARTHA : Somebody ought to tell her. If mother won't I must.

BARBARA : I'm extremely fond of Constance. Of course I've known what was going on for a long time and I've been dreadfully worried.

MARTHA : John has put her into an odious position. No man has the right to humiliate his wife as he has humiliated Constance. He's made her perfectly ridiculous.

MRS. CULVER : If women were ridiculous because their husbands are unfaithful to them there would surely be a great deal more merriment in the world than there is.

BARBARA [*Delighted to have a good gossip*] : You know they were lunching together to-day?

MARTHA : We hadn't heard that. But they were dining together the night before last.

MRS. CULVER [*Brightly*] : We know what they had to eat for dinner. Do you know what they had to eat for luncheon?

MARTHA : Mother.

MRS. CULVER : Well, I thought she seemed rather uppish about the lunch.

MARTHA : You have no sense of decency, mother.

MRS. CULVER : Oh, my dear, don't talk to me about decency. Decency died with dear Queen Victoria.

BARBARA [*To* MRS. CULVER] : But you can't approve of John having an open and flagrant intrigue with Constance's greatest friend.

MRS. CULVER : It may be that with advancing years my arteries have hardened. I am unable to attach any great importance to the philanderings of men. I think it's their nature. John is a very hard-working surgeon. If he likes to lunch and dine with a pretty woman now and then I don't think he's much to blame. It must be very tiresome to have three meals a day with the same woman for seven days a week. I'm a little bored myself at seeing Martha opposite me at the dinner-table. And men can't stand boredom as well as women.

MARTHA : I'm sure I'm very much obliged to you, mother.

BARBARA [*Significantly*]: But they're not only lunching and dining together.

MRS. CULVER: You fear the worst, my dear?

BARBARA [*With solemnity*]: I know the worst.

MRS. CULVER: I always think that's such a comfort. With closed doors and no one listening to us, so long as a man is kind and civil to his wife do you blame him very much if he strays occasionally from the narrow path of virtue?

MARTHA: Do you mean to say that you attach no importance to husbands and wives keeping their marriage vows?

MRS. CULVER: I think wives should.

BARBARA: But that's grossly unfair. Why should *they* any more than men?

MRS. CULVER: Because on the whole they like it. We ascribe a great deal of merit to ourselves because we're faithful to our husbands. I don't believe we deserve it for a minute. We're naturally faithful creatures and we're faithful because we have no particular inclination to be anything else.

BARBARA: I wonder.

MRS. CULVER: My dear, you are a widow and perfectly free. Have you really had any great desire to do anything that the world might say you shouldn't?

BARBARA: I have my business. When you work hard eight hours a day you don't much want to be bothered with love. In the evening the tired business woman wants to go to a musical comedy or play cards. She doesn't want to be worried with adoring males.

MARTHA: By the way, how is your business?

BARBARA: Growing by leaps and bounds. As a matter of fact I came here to-day to ask Constance if she would like to come in with me.

MRS. CULVER: Why should she? John earns plenty of money.

BARBARA: Well, I thought if things came to a crisis she might like to know that her independence was assured.

MRS. CULVER: Oh, you want them to come to a crisis too?

BARBARA: No, of course I don't. But, you know, they can't go on like this. It's a miracle that Constance hasn't heard yet. She's bound to find out soon.

MRS. CULVER: I suppose it's inevitable.

MARTHA: I hope she'll find out as quickly as possible. I still think it's mother's duty to tell her.

MRS. CULVER: Which I have no intention of doing.

MARTHA: And if mother won't I think I ought.

MRS. CULVER: Which I have no intention of permitting.

MARTHA: He's humiliated her beyond endurance. Her position is intolerable. I have no words to express my opinion of Marie-Louise, and the first time I see her I shall tell her exactly what I think of her. She's a horrid, ungrateful, mean and contemptible little cat.

BARBARA: Anyhow I think it would be a comfort to Constance to know that if anything happened she has me to turn to.

MRS. CULVER: But John would make her a handsome allowance. He's a very generous man.

MARTHA [*Indignantly*]: Do you think Constance would accept it?

BARBARA: Martha's quite right, Mrs. Culver. No woman in those circumstances would take a penny of his money.

MRS. CULVER: That's what she'd say. But she'd take care that her lawyer made the best arrangement he could. Few men know with what ingenuity we women can combine the disinterested gesture with a practical eye for the main chance.

BARBARA: Aren't you rather cynical, Mrs. Culver?

MRS. CULVER: I hope not. But when women are alone together I don't see why they shouldn't tell the truth now and then. It's a rest from the weary round of pretending to be something that we quite well know we're not.

MARTHA [*Stiffly*]: I'm not aware that I've ever pretended to be anything I wasn't.

MRS. CULVER: I dare say not, my dear. But I've always thought you were a little stupid. You take after your poor father. Constance and I have the brains of the family.

[CONSTANCE *comes into the room. She is a handsome woman of six and thirty. She has been out and wears a hat.*]

BARBARA [*Eagerly*]: Constance.

CONSTANCE: I'm so sorry I wasn't in. How nice of you all to wait. How are you, mother darling?

[*She kisses them one after another.*]

MARTHA: What have you been doing all day, Constance?

CONSTANCE: Oh, I've been shopping with Marie-Louise. She's just coming up.

BARBARA [*With dismay*]: Is she here?

CONSTANCE: Yes. She's telephoning.

MARTHA [*Ironically*]: You and Marie-Louise are quite inseparable.

CONSTANCE: I like her. She amuses me.

MARTHA: Were you lunching together?

CONSTANCE: No, she was lunching with a beau.

MARTHA [*With a glance at* MRS. CULVER]: Oh, really. [*Breezily*] John always comes home to luncheon, doesn't he?

CONSTANCE [*With great frankness*]: When he doesn't have to be at the hospital too early.

MARTHA: Was he lunching with you to-day?

CONSTANCE: No. He was engaged.

MARTHA: Where?

CONSTANCE: Good heavens, I don't know! When you've been married as long as I have you never ask your husband where he's going.

MARTHA: I don't know why not.

CONSTANCE [*Smiling*]: Because he might take it into his head to ask *you*.

MRS. CULVER: And also because if you're a wise woman you have confidence in your husband.

CONSTANCE: John has never given me a moment's uneasiness yet.

MARTHA: You're lucky.

CONSTANCE [*With her tongue in her cheek*]: Or wise.

[MARIE-LOUISE *appears. She is a very pretty little thing, beautifully dressed, of the clinging, large-eyed type.*]

MARIE-LOUISE: Oh, I didn't know there was a party.

MRS. CULVER: Martha and I are just going.

CONSTANCE: You know my mother, Marie-Louise.

MARIE-LOUISE: Of course I do.

CONSTANCE: She's a very nice mother.

MRS. CULVER: With her head screwed on the right way and very active for her years.

[MARIE-LOUISE *kisses* BARBARA *and* MARTHA.]

MARIE-LOUISE: How do you do.

MARTHA [*Looking at her dress*]: That's new, isn't it, Marie-Louise?

MARIE-LOUISE: Yes, I've never had it on before.

MARTHA: Oh, did you put it on because you were lunching with a beau?

MARIE-LOUISE: What makes you think I was lunching with a beau?

MARTHA: Constance told me so.

CONSTANCE: It was only a guess on my part. [*To* MARIE-LOUISE] When we met I noticed that your eyes were shining and you had that pleased, young look a woman always gets when some one has been telling her she's the most adorable thing in the world.

MARTHA: Tell us who it was, Marie-Louise.

CONSTANCE: Do nothing of the kind, Marie-Louise. Keep it a secret and give us something to gossip about.

BARBARA: How is your husband, dear?

MARIE-LOUISE: Oh, he's very well. I've just been telephoning to him.

BARBARA: I never saw any one adore his wife so obviously as he adores you.

MARIE-LOUISE: Yes, he's sweet, isn't he?

BARBARA: But doesn't it make you a little nervous sometimes? It must be nerve-racking to be obliged to live up to such profound devotion. It would be a dreadful shock if he ever found out that you were not everything he thought you.

CONSTANCE [*Charmingly*]: But Marie-Louise is everything he thinks her.

MARIE-LOUISE: And even if I weren't I think it would require more than the evidence of his eyes to persuade him.

CONSTANCE: Listen. There's John. [*She goes to the door and calls*] John! John!

JOHN [*Downstairs*]: Hulloa.

CONSTANCE: Are you coming up? Marie-Louise is here.

JOHN: Yes, I'm just coming.

CONSTANCE: He's been operating all the afternoon. I expect he's tired out.

MARTHA [*With a look at* MARIE-LOUISE]: I dare say he only had a sandwich for luncheon.

[JOHN *comes in. He is a tall, spare man of about forty.*]

JOHN: Good Lord, I never saw such a lot of people. How is my mother-in-law?

MRS. CULVER: Mother-in-lawish.

JOHN [*Kissing her—to* BARBARA]: You know, I only married Constance because her mother wouldn't have me.

MRS. CULVER: I was too young at the time to marry a boy twenty years younger than myself.

CONSTANCE: It hasn't prevented you from flirting outrageously with the creature ever since. It's lucky I'm not a jealous woman.

JOHN: What have you been doing all day, darling?

CONSTANCE: I've been shopping with Marie-Louise.

JOHN [*Shaking hands with* MARIE-LOUISE]: Oh, how do you do. Did you lunch together?

MARTHA: No, she lunched with a beau.

JOHN: I wish it had been me. [*To* MARIE-LOUISE] What have you been doing with yourself lately? We haven't seen you for ages.

MARIE-LOUISE: You're never about. Constance and I almost live in one another's pockets.

JOHN: How's that rich husband of yours?

MARIE-LOUISE: I've just been speaking to him. Isn't it a bore, he's got to go down to Birmingham for the night.

CONSTANCE: You'd better come and dine with us.

MARIE-LOUISE: Oh, it's awfully nice of you. But I'm tired out. I shall just go to bed and have an egg.

JOHN: I was just going to tell you, Constance. I shan't be in this evening. I've got an acute appendix to do.

CONSTANCE: Oh, what a nuisance.

MARTHA: You've got a wonderful profession, John. If you ever want to do anything or go anywhere you've only got to say you've got an operation and no one can prove it's a lie.

CONSTANCE: Oh, my dear, you mustn't put suspicions into my innocent head. It would never occur to John to be so deceitful. [*To* JOHN] Would it?

JOHN: I think I'd have to go an awful long way before I managed to deceive you, darling.

CONSTANCE [*With a little smile*]: Sometimes I think you're right.

MARIE-LOUISE: I do like to see a husband and wife so devoted to one another as you and John. You've been married fifteen years, haven't you?

JOHN: Yes. And it doesn't seem a day too much.

MARIE-LOUISE: Well, I must be running along. I'm late already. Good-bye, darling. Good-bye, Mrs. Culver.

CONSTANCE: Good-bye, darling. We've had such a nice afternoon.

MARIE-LOUISE [*Giving her hand to* JOHN]: Good-bye.

JOHN: Oh, I'll come downstairs with you.

MARTHA: I was just going, Marie-Louise. I'll come with you.

MARIE-LOUISE [*With presence of mind*]: John, I wonder if you'd mind looking at my knee for a minute. It's been rather painful for the last day or two.

JOHN: Of course not. Come into my consulting-room. These knee-caps are troublesome things when you once get them out of order.

MARTHA [*Firmly*]: I'll wait for you. You won't be long, will you? We might share a taxi.

MARIE-LOUISE: I've got my car.

MARTHA: Oh, how nice! You can give me a lift then.

MARIE-LOUISE: Of course. I shall be delighted.

[JOHN *opens the door for* MARIE-LOUISE. *She goes out and he follows her.* CONSTANCE *has watched this little scene coolly, but with an alert mind.*]

MARTHA: What is the matter with her knee?

CONSTANCE: It slips.

MARTHA: What happens then?

CONSTANCE: She slips too.

MARTHA: Are you never jealous of these women who come and see John in his consulting-room?

CONSTANCE: He always has a nurse within call in case they should attempt to take liberties with him.

MARTHA [*Amiably*]: Is the nurse there now?

CONSTANCE: And anyway I can't help thinking that the sort of woman who wants to be made love to in a consulting-room with a lively odour of antiseptics is the sort of woman who wears horrid undies. I could never bring myself to be jealous of her.

MARTHA: Marie-Louise gave me two of her chemises to copy only the other day.

CONSTANCE: Oh, did she give you the cerise one with the Irish lace insertions? I thought that sweet. I've copied that.

BARBARA: It's true that Marie-Louise is very pretty.

CONSTANCE: Marie-Louise is a darling. But she and John have known each other far too long. John likes her of course, but he says she has no brain.

MARTHA: Men don't always say what they think.

CONSTANCE: Fortunately, or we shouldn't always know what they feel.

MARTHA: Don't you think John has any secrets from you?

CONSTANCE: I'm sure of it. But of course a good wife always pretends not to know the little things her husband wishes to keep hidden from her. That is an elementary rule in matrimonial etiquette.

MARTHA: Don't forget that men were deceivers ever.

CONSTANCE: My dear, you talk like a confirmed spinster. What woman was ever deceived that didn't want to be? Do you really think that men are mysterious? They're children. Why, my dear, John at forty isn't nearly so grown up as Helen at fourteen.

BARBARA: How is your girl, Constance?

CONSTANCE: Oh, she's very well. She loves boarding-school, you know. They're like little boys, men. Sometimes of course they're rather naughty and you have to pretend to be angry with them. They attach so much importance to such entirely unimportant things that it's really touching. And they're so helpless. Have you never nursed a man when he's ill? It wrings your heart. It's just like a dog or a horse. They haven't got the sense to come in out of the rain, poor darlings. They have all the charming qualities that accompany general incompetence. They're sweet and good and silly, and tiresome and selfish. You can't help liking them, they're so ingenuous, and so simple. They have no complexity or finesse. I think they're sweet, but it's absurd to take them seriously. You're a wise woman, mother. What do you think?

MRS. CULVER: I think you're not in love with your husband.

CONSTANCE: What nonsense.

[JOHN *comes in.*]

JOHN: Marie-Louise is waiting for you, Martha. I've just put a little bandage round her knee.

CONSTANCE: I hope you weren't rough.

MARTHA [*To* CONSTANCE]: Good-bye, dear. Are you coming, mother?

MRS. CULVER: Not just yet.

MARTHA: Good-bye, Barbara.

[MARTHA *and* JOHN *go out.*]

BARBARA: Constance, I've got a suggestion to make to you. You know that my business has been growing by leaps and bounds and I simply cannot get along alone any more. I was wondering if you'd like to come in with me.

CONSTANCE: Oh, my dear, I'm not a business woman.

BARBARA: You've got marvellous taste and you have ideas. You could do all the decorating and I'd confine myself to buying and selling furniture.

CONSTANCE: But I've got no capital.

BARBARA: I've got all the capital I want. I must have help and I know no one more suitable than you. We'd go fifty-fifty and I think I can promise that you'd make a thousand to fifteen hundred a year.

CONSTANCE: I've been an idle woman so long. I think I'd find it dreadfully hard to work eight hours a day.

BARBARA: Won't you think it over? It's very interesting, you know. You're naturally energetic. Don't you get bored with doing nothing all the time?

CONSTANCE: I don't think John would like it. After all, it would look as though he couldn't afford to support me.

BARBARA: Oh, not nowadays surely. There's no reason that a woman shouldn't have a career just as much as a man.

CONSTANCE: I think my career is looking after John—running a house for him, entertaining his friends and making him happy and comfortable.

BARBARA: Don't you think it rather a mistake to put all your eggs in one basket? Supposing that career failed you?

CONSTANCE: Why should it?

BARBARA: Of course I hope it won't. But men, you know, are fluctuating and various. Independence is a very good thing, and a woman who stands on her own feet financially can look upon the future with a good deal of confidence.

CONSTANCE: It's sweet of you, but so long as John and I are happy together I think I should be a fool to do anything that would vex him.

BARBARA: Of course I'm in no immediate hurry. One never knows what the future will bring forth. I want you to know that if you change your mind the job is open to you. I don't think I shall ever find any one so competent as you. You have only to say the word.

CONSTANCE: Oh, Barbara, you are kind to me. It's a splendid offer and I'm ever so grateful to you. Don't think me horrid if I say I hope I shall never need to accept it.

BARBARA: Of course not. Good-bye, darling.

CONSTANCE: Good-bye, dear.

[*They kiss, and* BARBARA *goes out.* CONSTANCE *rings the bell.*]

MRS. CULVER: Are you quite happy, dear?

CONSTANCE: Oh, quite. Don't I look it?

MRS. CULVER: I'm bound to say you do. So far as I can judge by the look of you I should say you haven't a trouble in the world.

CONSTANCE: You'd be wrong. My cook has given notice and she makes the best meringues I've ever eaten.

MRS. CULVER: I like John.

CONSTANCE: So do I. He has all the solid qualities that

make a man a good husband, an agreeable temper, a sense of humour and an entire indifference to petty extravagance.

MRS. CULVER: How right you are, darling, to realise that those are the solid qualities.

CONSTANCE: It's not the seven deadly virtues that make a man a good husband, but the three hundred pleasing amiabilities.

MRS. CULVER: Of course one has to compromise in life. One has to make the best of things. One mustn't expect too much from people. If one wants to be happy in one's own way one must let others be happy in theirs. If one can't get this, that and the other the wise thing is to make up one's mind to do without it. The great thing is not to let vanity warp one's reasonable point of view.

CONSTANCE: Mother, mother, pull yourself together.

MRS. CULVER: Everybody's so clever nowadays. They see everything but the obvious. I've discovered that I only have to say it quite simply in order to be thought a most original and amusing old lady.

CONSTANCE: Spare me, darling.

MRS. CULVER [*Affectionately*]: If at any time anything went wrong with you, you would tell your mother, wouldn't you?

CONSTANCE: Of course.

MRS. CULVER: I hate the thought that you might be unhappy and let a foolish pride prevent you from letting me console and advise you.

CONSTANCE [*With feeling*]: It wouldn't, mother dear.

MRS. CULVER: I had rather an odd experience the other day. A little friend of mine came to see me and told me that her husband was neglecting her. I asked her why she told me and not her own mother. She said that her mother had never wanted her to marry and it would mortify her now to have to say that she had made a mistake.

CONSTANCE: Oh, well, John never neglects me, mother.

MRS. CULVER: Of course I gave her a good talking to. She didn't get much sympathy from me.

CONSTANCE [*With a smile*]: That was very unkind, wasn't it?

MRS. CULVER: I have my own ideas about marriage. If a man neglects his wife it's her own fault, and if he's systematically unfaithful to her in nine cases out of ten she only has herself to blame.

CONSTANCE [*Ringing the bell*]: Systematically is a grim word.

MRS. CULVER: No sensible woman attaches importance to an occasional slip. Time and chance are responsible for that.

CONSTANCE: And shall we say, masculine vanity?

MRS. CULVER: I told my little friend that if her husband was unfaithful to her it was because he found other women more attractive. Why should she be angry with him for that? Her business was to be more attractive than they.

CONSTANCE: You are not what they call a feminist, mother, are you?

MRS. CULVER: After all, what is fidelity?

CONSTANCE: Mother, do you mind if I open the window?

MRS. CULVER: It is open.

CONSTANCE: In that case do you mind if I shut it? I feel that when a woman of your age asks such a question I should make some sort of symbolic gesture.

MRS. CULVER: Don't be ridiculous. Of course I believe in fidelity for women. I suppose no one has ever questioned the desirability of that. But men are different. Women should remember that they have their homes and their name and position and their family, and they should learn to close their eyes when it's possible they may see something they are not meant to.

[*The butler comes in.*]

BENTLEY: Did you ring, Madam?

CONSTANCE: Yes. I am expecting Mr. Bernard Kersal. I'm not at home to anybody else.

BENTLEY: Very good, Madam.

CONSTANCE: Is Mr. Middleton in?

BENTLEY: Yes, Madam. He's in the consulting-room.

CONSTANCE: Very well.

[*The butler goes out.*]

MRS. CULVER: Is that a polite way of telling me that I had better take myself off?

CONSTANCE: Of course not. On the contrary I particularly want you to stay.

MRS. CULVER: Who is this mysterious gentleman?

CONSTANCE: Mother. Bernard.

MRS. CULVER: That says nothing to me at all. Not Saint Bernard, darling?

CONSTANCE: Pull yourself together, my pet. You must remember Bernard Kersal. He proposed to me.

MRS. CULVER: Oh, my dear, you cannot expect me to remember the names of all the young men who proposed to you.

CONSTANCE: Yes, but he proposed more than any of the others.

MRS. CULVER: Why?

CONSTANCE: I suppose because I refused him. I can't think of any other reason.

MRS. CULVER: He made no impression on me.

CONSTANCE: I don't suppose he tried to.

MRS. CULVER: What did he look like?

CONSTANCE: He was tall.

MRS. CULVER: They were all tall.

CONSTANCE: He had brown hair and brown eyes.

MRS. CULVER: They all had brown hair and brown eyes.

CONSTANCE: He danced divinely.

MRS. CULVER: They all danced divinely.

CONSTANCE: I very nearly married him, you know.

MRS. CULVER: Why didn't you?

CONSTANCE: I think he was a trifle too much inclined to lie down on the floor and let me walk over him.

MRS. CULVER: In short he had no sense of humour.

CONSTANCE: I was quite certain that he loved me, and I was never absolutely sure that John did.

MRS. CULVER: Well, you're sure now, dear, aren't you?

CONSTANCE: Oh, yes. John adores me.

MRS. CULVER: And what's this young man coming for to-day?

CONSTANCE: He's not such a very young man any more. He was twenty-nine then and so he must be nearly forty-five now.

MRS. CULVER: He isn't still in love with you?

CONSTANCE: I shouldn't think so. Do you think it possible after fifteen years? It's surely very unlikely. Don't look at me like that, mother. I don't like it.

MRS. CULVER: Don't talk stuff and nonsense to me, child. Of course you know if he's in love with you or not.

CONSTANCE: But I haven't seen him since I married John. You see he lives in Japan. He's a merchant or something in Kobe. He was here during the war on leave. But that was when I was so dreadfully ill and I didn't see him.

MRS. CULVER: Oh! Why's he here now then? Have you been corresponding with him?

CONSTANCE: No. One can't write letters to any one one never sees for fifteen years. He always sends me flowers on my birthday.

MRS. CULVER: That's rather sweet of him.

CONSTANCE: And the other day I had a letter from him saying he was in England and would like to see me. So I asked him to come to-day.

MRS. CULVER: I wondered why you were so smart.

CONSTANCE: Of course he may be terribly changed. Men go off so dreadfully, don't they? He may be bald and fat now.

MRS. CULVER: He may be married.

CONSTANCE: Oh, if he were I don't think he'd want to come and see me, would he?

MRS. CULVER: I see you're under the impression that he's still in love with you.

CONSTANCE: Oh, I'm not.

MRS. CULVER: Then why are you so nervous?

CONSTANCE: It's only natural that I shouldn't want him to think me old and haggard. He adored me, mother. I suppose he still thinks of me as I was then. It wouldn't be very nice if his face fell about a yard and a half when he came into the room.

MRS. CULVER: I think I'd much better leave you to face the ordeal alone.

CONSTANCE: Oh, no, mother, you must stay. I particularly want you. You see, he may be awful and I may wish I'd never seen him again. It'll be so much easier if you're here. I may not want to be alone with him at all.

MRS. CULVER: Oh.

CONSTANCE [*With a twinkle in her eye*]: On the other hand I may.

MRS. CULVER: It seems to me you're putting me in a slightly embarrassing situation.

CONSTANCE: Now listen. If I think he's awful we'll just talk about the weather and the crops for a few minutes and then we'll have an ominous pause and stare at him. That always makes a man feel a perfect fool and the moment a man feels a fool he gets up and goes.

MRS. CULVER: Sometimes they don't know how to, poor dears, and the earth will never open and swallow them up.

CONSTANCE: On the other hand if I think he looks rather nice I shall just take out my handkerchief and carelessly place it on the piano.

MRS. CULVER: Why?

CONSTANCE: Darling, in order that you may rise to your aged feet and say, well, you really must be running along.

MRS. CULVER: Yes, I know that, but why should you carelessly place your handkerchief on the piano?

CONSTANCE: Because I am a creature of impulse. I shall have an impulse to place my handkerchief on the piano.

MRS. CULVER: Oh, very well. But I always mistrust impulses.

[BENTLEY *enters and announces* BERNARD KERSAL. *He is a tall good-looking man, sunburned and of healthy appearance. He is evidently very fit and he carries his forty-five years well.*]

BENTLEY: Mr. Kersal.

CONSTANCE: How do you do. Do you remember my mother?

BERNARD [*Shaking hands with her*]: I'm sure she doesn't remember me.

[CONSTANCE *takes a small handkerchief out of her bag.*]

MRS. CULVER: That is the soft answer that turneth away wrath.

CONSTANCE: It's rather late for tea, isn't it? Would you like a drink?

[*As she says this she goes towards the bell and places her handkerchief on the piano.*]

BERNARD: No, thanks. I've just this moment had one.

CONSTANCE: To brace you for seeing me?

BERNARD: I was nervous.

CONSTANCE: Have I changed as much as you expected?

BERNARD: Oh, that's not what I was nervous about.

MRS. CULVER: Is it really fifteen years since you saw Constance?

BERNARD: Yes. I didn't see her when I was last in England. When I got demobbed I had to go out to Japan again and get my business together. I haven't had a chance to come home before.

[CONSTANCE *has been giving her mother significant looks, but her mother does not notice them.* CONSTANCE *takes a second handkerchief out of her bag and when the opportunity arises places it neatly on the piano beside the first one.*]

MRS. CULVER: And are you home for long?

BERNARD: A year.

MRS. CULVER: Have you brought your wife with you?

BERNARD: I'm not married.

MRS. CULVER: Oh, Constance said you were married to a Japanese lady.

CONSTANCE: Nonsense, mother. I never said anything of the sort.

MRS. CULVER: Oh, perhaps I was thinking of Julia Linton. She married an Egyptian pasha. I believe she's very happy. At all events he hasn't killed her yet.

BERNARD: How is your husband?

CONSTANCE: He's very well. I dare say he'll be in presently.

BERNARD: Haven't you got a little sister? I suppose she's out now?

MRS. CULVER: He means Martha. She's come out and gone in again.

CONSTANCE: She was not so very much younger than me, you know. She's thirty-two now.

[MRS. CULVER *has taken no notice of the handkerchiefs and in desperation* CONSTANCE *takes a third from her bag and places it beside the other two.*]

MRS. CULVER: Do you like the East, Mr. Kersal?

BERNARD: One has a pretty good time there, you know.

[*Now* MRS. CULVER *catches sight of the three handkerchiefs and starts.*]

MRS. CULVER: I wonder what the time is.

CONSTANCE: It's late, mother. Are you dining out to-night? I suppose you want to have a lie-down before you dress for dinner.

MRS. CULVER: I hope I shall see you again, Mr. Kersal.

BERNARD: Thank you very much.

[CONSTANCE *accompanies her to the door.*]

MRS. CULVER: Good-bye, darling. [*In a whisper*] I couldn't remember if the handkerchiefs meant go or stay.

CONSTANCE: You had only to use your eyes. You can see at a glance that he is the kind of man one would naturally want to have a heart-to-heart talk with after fifteen years.

MRS. CULVER: You only confused me by putting more and more handkerchiefs on the piano.

CONSTANCE: For goodness' sake, go, mother. [*Aloud*] Good-bye, my sweet. I'm sorry you've got to run away so soon.

MRS. CULVER: Good-bye.

[*She goes out and* CONSTANCE *comes back into the room.*]

CONSTANCE: Did you think it very rude of us to whisper? Mother has a passion for secrets.

BERNARD: Of course not.

CONSTANCE: Now let's sit down and make ourselves comfortable. Let me look at you. You haven't changed much. You're a little thinner and perhaps a little more lined. Men are so lucky, if they have any character they grow better-looking as they grow older. Do you know I'm thirty-six now?

BERNARD: What does that matter?

CONSTANCE: Shall I tell you something? When you wrote

and suggested coming here I was delighted at the thought of seeing you again and wrote at once making a date. And then I was panic-stricken. I would have given almost anything not to have sent that letter. And all to-day I've had such a horrible feeling at the pit of my stomach. Didn't you see my knees wobble when you came into the room?

BERNARD: In God's name, why?

CONSTANCE: Oh, my dear, I think you must be a little stupid. I should be a perfect fool if I didn't know that when I was a girl I was very pretty. It's rather a pang when you are forced to the conclusion that you're not quite so pretty as you were. People don't tell one. One tries to hide it from oneself. Anyhow I thought I'd rather know the worst. That's one of the reasons I asked you to come.

BERNARD: Whatever I thought you can hardly imagine that I should be deliberately rude.

CONSTANCE: Of course not. But I watched your face. I was afraid I'd see there: By God, how she's gone off.

BERNARD: And did you?

CONSTANCE: You were rather shy when you came in. You weren't thinking of me.

BERNARD: It's quite true, fifteen years ago you were a pretty girl. Now you're lovely. You're ten times more beautiful than you were then.

CONSTANCE: It's nice of you to say so.

BERNARD: Don't you believe it?

CONSTANCE: I think you do. And I confess that's sufficiently gratifying. Now tell me, why aren't you married? It's time you did, you know, or it'll be too late. You'll have a very lonely old age if you don't.

BERNARD: I never wanted to marry any one but you.

CONSTANCE: Oh, come, you're not going to tell me that you've never been in love since you were in love with me?

BERNARD: No, I've been in love half a dozen times, but when it came to the point I found I still loved you best.

CONSTANCE: I like you for saying that. I shouldn't have believed it if you'd said you'd never loved anybody else and I should have been vexed with you for thinking me such a fool as to believe it.

BERNARD: You see, it was you I loved in the others. One because she had hair like yours and another because her smile reminded me of your smile.

CONSTANCE: I hate to think that I've made you unhappy.

BERNARD: But you haven't. I've had a very good time; I've enjoyed my work; I've made a bit of money and I've had a lot of fun. I don't blame you for having married John instead of me.

CONSTANCE: Do you remember John?

BERNARD: Of course I do. He was a very nice fellow. I dare say he's made you a better husband than I should have. I've had my ups and downs. I'm very irritable sometimes. John's been able to give you everything you wanted. You were much safer with him. By the way, I suppose I can still call you Constance.

CONSTANCE: Of course. Why not? Do you know, I think you have a very nice nature, Bernard.

BERNARD: Are you happy with John?

CONSTANCE: Oh, very. I don't say that he has never given me a moment's uneasiness. He did once, but I took hold of myself and saw that I mustn't be silly. I'm very glad I did. I think I can quite honestly say that ours has been a very happy and successful marriage.

BERNARD: I'm awfully glad to hear that. Do you think it's cheek to ask if John loves you?

CONSTANCE: I'm sure he loves me.

BERNARD: And do you love him?

CONSTANCE: Very much.

BERNARD: May I make you a short speech?

CONSTANCE: If I may interrupt at suitable moments.

BERNARD: I hope you're going to let me see a great deal of you during this year I've got at home.

CONSTANCE: I want to see a great deal of you.

BERNARD: There's just one thing I want to get off my chest and then I needn't refer to it again. I am just as madly in love with you as I was when I asked you to marry me fifteen years ago. I think I shall remain in love with you all my life. I'm too old a dog to learn new tricks. But I want you to know that you needn't have the smallest fear that I shall make a nuisance of myself. I should think it an awfully caddish thing to try to come between you and John. I suppose we all want to be happy, but I don't believe the best way of being that is to try to upset other people's happiness.

CONSTANCE: That's not such a very long speech after all. At a public dinner they would hardly even call it a few remarks.

BERNARD: All I ask for is your friendship and if in return I care to give you my love I don't see that it's any one's business but my own.

CONSTANCE: I don't think it is. I think I can be a very good friend, Bernard.

[*The door opens and* JOHN *comes in.*]

JOHN: Oh, I'm sorry. I didn't know you were engaged.

CONSTANCE: I'm not. Come in. This is Bernard Kersal.

JOHN: How do you do?

BERNARD: I'm afraid you don't remember me.

JOHN: If you ask me point-blank I think it's safer to confess I don't.

CONSTANCE: Don't be so silly, John. He used to come to mother's.

JOHN: Before we were married, d'you mean?

CONSTANCE: Yes. You spent several week-ends with us together.

JOHN: My dear, that was fifteen years ago. I'm awfully sorry not to remember you, but I'm delighted to see you now.

CONSTANCE: He's just come back from Japan.

JOHN: Oh, well, I hope we shall see you again. I'm just going along to the club to have a rubber before dinner, darling. [*To* BERNARD] Why don't you dine here with Constance? I've got an acute appendix and she'll be all alone, poor darling.

BERNARD: Oh, that's awfully kind of you.

CONSTANCE: It would be a friendly act. Are you free?

BERNARD: Always to do a friendly act.

CONSTANCE: Very well. I shall expect you at eight-fifteen.

THE END OF ACT ONE

ACT TWO

The Scene is the same as in the First Act.
    A fortnight has passed.
    MARTHA *in walking costume and a hat is looking at an illustrated paper.*
    BENTLEY *comes in.*

BENTLEY: Mr. Kersal is here, Miss.

MARTHA: Oh! Ask him if he won't come up.

BENTLEY: Very good, Miss. [*He goes out and in a moment comes in again to announce* BERNARD, *and then goes*] Mr. Kersal.

MARTHA: Constance is dressing. She won't be very long.

BERNARD: Oh, I see. Well, there's no violent hurry.

MARTHA: You're taking her to Ranelagh, aren't you?

BERNARD: That was the idea. I know some of the fellows who are playing to-day.

MARTHA: Are you having a good time in London?

BERNARD: Marvellous. When a man's lived in the East as long as I have, he's apt to feel rather out of it when he comes home. But Constance and John have been ripping to me.

MARTHA: Do you like John?

BERNARD: Yes. He's been awfully kind.

MARTHA: Do you know, I remember you quite well.

BERNARD: Oh, you can't. You were a kid when I used to come down and stay with your mother.

MARTHA: I was sixteen. Do you imagine I wasn't thrilled to the marrow by Constance's young men?

BERNARD: There were a good many of them. I should have thought your marrow got callous.

MARTHA: But you were one of the serious ones. I always thought you terribly romantic.

BERNARD: I was terribly romantic. I think it's becoming in the young.

MARTHA: I don't think it's unbecoming in the not quite as young.

BERNARD: Don't think I'm romantic now. I make a considerable income and I'm putting on weight. The price of silk has ousted love's young dream in my manly bosom.

MARTHA: You're an unconscionable liar.

BERNARD: To which I can only retort that you're excessively rude.

MARTHA: You were madly in love with Constance in those days, weren't you?

BERNARD: You know, it's so long ago I forget.

MARTHA: I advised her to marry you rather than John.

BERNARD: Why?

MARTHA: Well, for one thing you lived in Japan. I would have married any one who would take me there.

BERNARD: I live there still.

MARTHA: Oh, I don't want to marry you.

BERNARD: I couldn't help suspecting that.

MARTHA: I could never really quite understand what she saw in John.

BERNARD: I suppose she loved him.

MARTHA: I wonder if she ever regrets that she married John rather than you.

BERNARD: Well, don't. She's perfectly satisfied with John and wouldn't change him for anything in the world.

MARTHA: It's exasperating, isn't it?

BERNARD: I don't think so. It must make it much more comfortable for a husband and wife to be content with one another.

MARTHA: You're in love with her still, aren't you?

BERNARD: Not a bit.

MARTHA: Upon my soul, you've got a nerve. Why, you donkey, you're giving it away all the time. Do you know what you look like when she's in the room? Have you any idea how your eyes change when they rest on her? When you speak her name it sounds as though you were kissing it.

BERNARD: I thought you were an odious child when you were sixteen, Martha, and now that you're thirty-two I think you're a horrible woman.

MARTHA: I'm not really. But I'm very fond of Constance and I'm inclined to be rather fond of you.

BERNARD: Don't you think you could show your attachment by minding your own business?

MARTHA: Why does it make you angry because I've told you that no one can see you with Constance for five minutes without knowing that you adore her?

BERNARD: My dear, I'm here for one year. I want to be happy. I don't want to give trouble or cause trouble. I value my friendship with Constance and I hate the idea that anything should interfere with it.

MARTHA: Hasn't it occurred to you that she may want more than your friendship?

BERNARD: No, it has not.

MARTHA: You need not jump down my throat.

BERNARD: Constance is perfectly happy with her husband. You must think me a damned swine if you think I'm going to butt in and try to smash up a perfectly wonderful union.

MARTHA: But, you poor fool, don't you know that John has been notoriously unfaithful to Constance for ages?

BERNARD: I don't believe it.

MARTHA: Ask any one you like. Mother knows it. Barbara Fawcett knows it. Every one knows it but Constance.

BERNARD: That certainly isn't true. Mrs. Durham told me when I met her at dinner two or three days ago that John and Constance were the most devoted couple she'd ever known.

MARTHA: Did Marie-Louise tell you that?

BERNARD: She did.

[MARTHA *begins to laugh. She can hardly restrain herself.*]

MARTHA: The nerve. Marie-Louise. Oh, my poor Bernard. Marie-Louise is John's mistress.

BERNARD: Marie-Louise is Constance's greatest friend.

MARTHA: Yes.

BERNARD: If this is a pack of lies I swear I'll damned well wring your neck.

MARTHA: All right.

BERNARD: That was a silly thing to say. I'm sorry.

MARTHA: Oh, I don't mind. I like a man to be violent. I think you're just the sort of man Constance needs.

BERNARD: What the devil do you mean by that?

MARTHA: It can't go on. Constance is being made perfectly ridiculous. Her position is monstrous. I thought she ought to be told and as every one else seemed to shirk the job I was prepared to do it myself. My mother was so disagreeable about it, I've had to promise not to say a word.

BERNARD: You're not under the delusion that I'm going to tell her?

MARTHA: No, I don't really think it would come very well from you. But things can't go on. She's bound to find out. All I want you to do is to . . . well, stand by.

BERNARD: But Marie-Louise has got a husband. What about him?

MARTHA: His only ambition in life is to make a million. He's the sort of a fool who thinks a woman loves him just because he loves her. Marie-Louise can turn him round her little finger.

BERNARD: Has Constance never suspected?

MARTHA: Never. You've only got to look at her. Really, her self-confidence sometimes is positively maddening.

BERNARD: I wonder if it wouldn't be better that she never did find out. She's so happy. She's entirely carefree. You've only got to look at that open brow and those frank, trustful eyes.

MARTHA: I thought you loved her.

BERNARD: Enough to want her happiness above all things.

MARTHA: You *are* forty-five, aren't you? I forgot that for a moment.

BERNARD: Dear Martha. You have such an attractive way of putting things.

[CONSTANCE'S *voice on the stairs is heard calling:*
    BENTLEY, BENTLEY.]

MARTHA: Oh, there's Constance. I can't imagine where mother is. I think I'll go into the brown room and write a letter.

[BERNARD *takes no notice of what she says nor does he
    make any movement when she goes out. A moment
    later* CONSTANCE *comes in.*]

CONSTANCE: Have I kept you waiting?

BERNARD: It doesn't matter.

CONSTANCE: Hulloa! What's up?

BERNARD: With me? Nothing. Why?

CONSTANCE: You look all funny. Why are your eyes suddenly opaque?

BERNARD: I didn't know they were.

CONSTANCE: Are you trying to hide something from me?

BERNARD: Of course not.

CONSTANCE: Have you had bad news from Japan?

BERNARD: No. Far from it. Silk is booming.

CONSTANCE: Then you're going to tell me that you've just got engaged to a village maiden.

BERNARD: No, I'm not.

CONSTANCE: I hate people who keep secrets from me.

BERNARD: I have no secrets from you.

CONSTANCE: Do you think I don't know your face by now?

BERNARD: You'll make me vain. I would never have ventured to think that you took the trouble to look twice at my ugly face.

CONSTANCE [*With sudden suspicion*]: Wasn't Martha here when you came? She hasn't gone, has she?

BERNARD: She's waiting for her mother. She's gone into another room to write letters.

CONSTANCE: Did you see her?

BERNARD [*Trying to be very casual*]: Yes. We had a little chat about the weather.

CONSTANCE [*Immediately grasping what has happened*]: Oh—— Don't you think we ought to be starting?

BERNARD: There's plenty of time. It's no good getting there too early.

CONSTANCE: Then I'll take off my hat.

BERNARD: And it's jolly here, isn't it? I love your room.

CONSTANCE: Do you think it's a success? I did it myself. Barbara Fawcett wants me to go into the decorating business. She's in it, you know, and she's making quite a lot of money.

BERNARD [*Smiling to hide his anxiety in asking the question*]: Aren't you happy at home?

CONSTANCE [*Breezily*]: I don't think it necessarily means

one's unhappy at home because one wants an occupation. One may very easily grow tired of going to parties all the time. But as a matter of fact I refused Barbara's offer.

BERNARD [*Insisting*]: You are happy, aren't you?

CONSTANCE: Very.

BERNARD: You've made *me* very happy during this last fortnight. I feel as though I'd never been away. You've been awfully kind to me.

CONSTANCE: I'm very glad you think so. I don't know that I've done anything very much for you.

BERNARD: Yes, you have. You've let me see you.

CONSTANCE: I let the policeman at the corner do that, you know.

BERNARD: You mustn't think that because I take care only to talk to you of quite casual things I don't still love you with all my heart.

CONSTANCE [*Quite coolly*]: We agreed when first you came back that your feelings were entirely your business.

BERNARD: Do you mind my loving you?

CONSTANCE: Oughtn't we all to love one another?

BERNARD: Don't tease me.

CONSTANCE: My dear, I can't help being pleased and flattered and rather touched. It is rather wonderful that any one should care for me. . . .

BERNARD [*Interrupting*]: So much—?

CONSTANCE: After so many years.

BERNARD: If any one had asked me fifteen years ago if I could love you more than I loved you then I should have said it was impossible. I love you ten times more than I ever loved you before.

CONSTANCE [*Going on with her own speech*]: But I don't in the least want you to make love to me now.

BERNARD: I know. I'm not going to. I know you far too well.

CONSTANCE [*Amused and a trifle taken aback*]: I don't quite know what you've been doing for the last five minutes.

BERNARD: I was merely stating a few plain facts.

CONSTANCE: Oh, I beg your pardon. I thought it was something quite different. I'm afraid you might mistake my meaning if I said I'm quite curious to see how you *do* make love.

BERNARD [*Good-humouredly*] : I have a notion that you're laughing at me.

CONSTANCE : In the hope of teaching you to laugh at yourself.

BERNARD : I've been very good during the last fortnight, haven't I?

CONSTANCE : Yes, I kept on saying to myself, I wonder if a pat of butter really would melt in his mouth.

BERNARD : Well, for just a minute I'm going to let myself go.

CONSTANCE : I wouldn't if I were you.

BERNARD : Yes, but you're not. I want to tell you just once that I worship the ground you tread on. There's never been any one in the world for me but you.

CONSTANCE : Oh, nonsense. There have been half a dozen. We are seven.

BERNARD : They were all you. I love you with all my heart. I admire you more than any woman I've ever met. I respect you. I'm an awful fool when it comes to the point. I don't know how to say all I've got in my heart without feeling like a perfect ass. I love you. I want you to know that if ever you're in trouble I should look upon it as the greatest possible happiness to be allowed to help you.

CONSTANCE : That's very kind of you. I don't see why I should be in any great trouble.

BERNARD : Always and in all circumstances you can count on me absolutely. I will do anything in the world for you. If ever you want me you have only to give me a sign. I should be proud and happy to give my life for you.

CONSTANCE : It's sweet of you to say so.

BERNARD : Don't you believe it?

CONSTANCE [*With a charming smile*] : Yes.

BERNARD : I should like to think that it meant—oh, not very much, but just a little to you.

CONSTANCE [*Almost shaken*] : It means a great deal. I thank you.

BERNARD : Now we won't say anything more about it.

CONSTANCE [*Recovering her accustomed coolness*]: But why did you think it necessary to say all this just now?

BERNARD: I wanted to get it off my chest.

CONSTANCE: Oh, really.

BERNARD: You're not angry with me?

CONSTANCE: Oh, Bernard, I'm not that kind of a fool at all. . . . It's a pity that Martha doesn't marry.

BERNARD: Don't think that I'm going to marry her.

CONSTANCE: I don't. I merely thought that a husband would be a pleasant and useful occupation for her. She's quite a nice girl, you know. A liar, of course, but otherwise all right.

BERNARD: Oh?

CONSTANCE: Yes, a terrible liar, even for a woman. . . . Shall we start now? It's no good getting there when the polo is over.

BERNARD: All right. Let's start.

CONSTANCE: I'll put my hat on again. By the way, you haven't had a taxi waiting all this time, have you?

BERNARD: No, I've got a car. I thought I'd like to drive you down myself.

CONSTANCE: Open or shut?

BERNARD: Open.

CONSTANCE: Oh, my dear, then I must get another hat. A broad brim like this is such a bore in an open car.

BERNARD: Oh, I'm sorry.

CONSTANCE: It doesn't matter a bit. I shall only be a minute. And why on earth shouldn't one be comfortable if one can!

[*She goes out. In a moment* BENTLEY *shows in* MARIE-LOUISE.]

MARIE-LOUISE: Oh, how do you do. [*To* BENTLEY] Will you tell Mr. Middleton at once?

BENTLEY: Yes, Madam.

[*Exit* BENTLEY.]

MARIE-LOUISE [*Rather flustered*]: I particularly wanted to see John for a minute and there are patients waiting to see him, so I asked Bentley if he couldn't come here.

Mortimer: Do you recognize this? I found it under my wife's pillow last night.

Constance: Oh, I am relieved. I couldn't make out where
I'd left it. Thank you so much.

BERNARD: I'll take myself off.

MARIE-LOUISE: I'm awfully sorry, but it's rather urgent. John hates to be disturbed like this.

BERNARD: I'll go into the next room.

MARIE-LOUISE: Are you waiting for Constance?

BERNARD: Yes, I'm taking her to Ranelagh. She's changing her hat.

MARIE-LOUISE: I see. Bentley told me she was upstairs. Good-bye. I shall only be a minute. [BERNARD *goes into the adjoining room just as* JOHN *comes in*] Oh, John, I'm sorry to drag you away from your patients.

JOHN: There's nothing urgent. They can wait for a few minutes. [BERNARD *has closed the door behind him, and* JOHN'S *tone changes. They speak now in a low voice and quickly*] Is anything the matter?

MARIE-LOUISE: Mortimer.

JOHN: What about Mortimer?

MARIE-LOUISE: I'm convinced he suspects.

JOHN: Why?

MARIE-LOUISE: He was so funny last night. He came into my room to say good-night to me. He sat on my bed. He was chatting nicely and he was asking what I'd been doing with myself all the evening. . . .

JOHN: Presumably you didn't tell him.

MARIE-LOUISE: No, I said I'd been dining here. And suddenly he got up and just said good-night and went out. His voice was so strange that I couldn't help looking at him. He was as red as a turkey cock.

JOHN: Is that all?

MARIE-LOUISE: He never came in to say good-morning to me before he went to the City.

JOHN: He may have been in a hurry.

MARIE-LOUISE: He's never in too much of a hurry for that.

JOHN: I think you're making a mountain of a mole heap.

MARIE-LOUISE: Don't be stupid, John. Can't you see I'm as nervous as a cat?

JOHN: I can. But I'm trying to persuade you there's nothing to be nervous about.

MARIE-LOUISE: What fools men are. They never will see

that it's the small things that matter. I tell you I'm frightened out of my wits.

JOHN: You know there's a devil of a distance between suspicion and proof.

MARIE-LOUISE: Oh, I don't think he could prove anything. But he can make himself awfully unpleasant. Supposing he put ideas in Constance's head?

JOHN: She'd never believe him.

MARIE-LOUISE: If the worst came to worst I could manage Mortimer. He's awfully in love with me. That always gives one such an advantage over a man.

JOHN: Of course you can twist Mortimer round your little finger.

MARIE-LOUISE: I should die of shame if Constance knew. After all, she's my greatest friend and I'm absolutely devoted to her.

JOHN: Constance is a peach. Of course I don't believe there's anything in this at all, but if there were, I'd be in favour of making a clean breast of it to Constance.

MARIE-LOUISE: Never!

JOHN: I expect she'd kick up a row. Any woman would. But she'd do anything in the world to help us out.

MARIE-LOUISE: A lot you know about women. She'd help you out, I dare say. But she'd stamp on me with both feet. That's only human nature.

JOHN: Not Constance's.

MARIE-LOUISE: Upon my word, it's lucky I'm fairly sure of you, John, or the way you talk of Constance would really make me jealous.

JOHN: Thank God you can smile. You're getting your nerve back.

MARIE-LOUISE: It's been a comfort to talk it over. It doesn't seem so bad now.

JOHN: I'm sure you've got nothing to be frightened about.

MARIE-LOUISE: I dare say it was only my fancy. It was a stupid risk to take all the same.

JOHN: Perhaps. Why did you look so devilish pretty?

MARIE-LOUISE: Oughtn't you to be getting back to your wretched patients?

JOHN: I suppose so. Will you stop and see Constance?

MARIE-LOUISE: I may as well. It would look rather odd if I went away without saying how d'you do to her.

JOHN [*Going*]: I'll leave you then. And don't worry.

MARIE-LOUISE: I won't. I dare say it was only a guilty conscience. I'll go and have my hair washed.

[*As* JOHN *is about to go,* MARTHA *comes in followed by* BERNARD.]

MARTHA [*With an almost exaggerated cordiality*]: I had no idea you were here, Marie-Louise.

MARIE-LOUISE: It's not very important.

MARTHA: I was just writing letters, waiting for mother, and Bernard's only just told me.

MARIE-LOUISE: I wanted to see John about something.

MARTHA: I hope you haven't got anything the matter with you, darling.

MARIE-LOUISE: No. Mortimer's been looking rather run-down lately and I want John to persuade him to take a holiday.

MARTHA: Oh, I should have thought he'd be more likely to take a physician's advice than a surgeon's in a thing like that.

MARIE-LOUISE: He's got a tremendous belief in John, you know.

MARTHA: In which I'm sure he's justified. John is so very reliable.

JOHN: What can I do for you, Martha? If you'd like me to cut out an appendix or a few tonsils I shall be happy to oblige you.

MARTHA: My dear John, you've only left me the barest necessities of existence as it is. I don't think I could manage with anything less than I have.

JOHN: My dear, as long as a woman has a leg to stand on she need not despair of exciting her surgeon's sympathy and interest.

[CONSTANCE *comes in with* MRS. CULVER.]

MARIE-LOUISE [*Kissing her*]: Darling.

CONSTANCE: How is your knee, still slipping?

MARIE-LOUISE: It always gives me more or less trouble, you know.

CONSTANCE: Yes, of course. I think you're very patient. In your place I should be furious with John. Of course I would never dream of consulting him if I had anything the matter with me.

MRS. CULVER: I'm sorry I've been so long, Martha. Have you been very impatient?

MARTHA: No, I've been passing the time very pleasantly.

MRS. CULVER: For others, darling, or only for yourself?

CONSTANCE: I met mother on the stairs and she came up with me while I changed my hat. Bernard is taking me down to Ranelagh.

JOHN: Oh, that'll be jolly.

BERNARD: We shall be dreadfully late.

CONSTANCE: Does it matter?

BERNARD: No.

[BENTLEY *comes in with a card on a small salver and takes it to* CONSTANCE. *She looks at the card and hesitates.*]

CONSTANCE: How very odd.

JOHN: What's the matter, Constance?

CONSTANCE: Nothing. [*For an instant she reflects*] Is he downstairs?

BENTLEY: Yes, Madam.

CONSTANCE: I don't know why he should send up a card. Show him up.

BENTLEY: Very good, Madam.

[*Exit* BENTLEY.]

JOHN: Who is it, Constance?

CONSTANCE: Come and sit down, Marie-Louise.

MARIE-LOUISE: I must go and so must you.

CONSTANCE: There's plenty of time. Do you like this hat?

MARIE-LOUISE: Yes. I think it's sweet.

CONSTANCE: What are *you* doing here, John? Haven't you got any patients to-day?

JOHN: Yes, there are two or three waiting. I'm just going down. As a matter of fact I thought I deserved a cigarette. [*He puts his hand to his hip pocket*] Hang, I've mislaid my cigarette case. You haven't seen it about, Constance?

CONSTANCE: No, I haven't.

JOHN: I looked for it everywhere this morning. I can't think where I left it. I must ring up the nursing-home and ask if I left it there.

CONSTANCE: I hope you haven't lost it.

JOHN: Oh, no. I'm sure I haven't. I've just put it somewhere.

[*The door opens and* BENTLEY *announces the visitor.*]

BENTLEY: Mr. Mortimer Durham.

MARIE-LOUISE [*Startled out of her wits*]: Oh!

CONSTANCE [*Quickly, seizing her wrist*]: Sit still, you fool. [MORTIMER DURHAM *comes in. He is a stoutish, biggish man of about forty, with a red face and an irascible manner. At the moment he is a prey to violent emotion.* BENTLEY *goes out*] Hulloa, Mortimer. What are you doing in these parts at this hour? Why on earth did you send up a card?

[*He stops and looks around.*]

MARIE-LOUISE: What is the matter, Mortimer?

MORTIMER [*To* CONSTANCE, *with difficulty restraining his fury*]: I thought you might like to know that your husband is my wife's lover.

MARIE-LOUISE: Morty!

CONSTANCE [*Keeping a firm hand on* MARIE-LOUISE *and very coolly to* MORTIMER]: Oh? What makes you think that?

MORTIMER [*Taking a gold cigarette case out of his pocket*]: Do you recognize this? I found it under my wife's pillow last night.

CONSTANCE: Oh, I am relieved. I couldn't make out where I'd left it. [*Taking it from him*] Thank you so much.

MORTIMER [*Angrily*]: It's not yours.

CONSTANCE: Indeed it is. I was sitting on Marie-Louise's bed and I must have slipped it under the pillow without thinking.

MORTIMER: It has John's initials on it.

CONSTANCE: I know. It was presented to him by a grateful patient and I thought it much too nice for him, so I just took it.

MORTIMER: What sort of fool do you take me for, Constance?

CONSTANCE: My dear Morty, why should I say it was my cigarette case if it wasn't?

MORTIMER: They had dinner together.

CONSTANCE: My poor Morty, I know that. You were going to a City banquet or something, and Marie-Louise rang up and asked if she might come and take potluck with us.

MORTIMER: Do you mean to say she dined here?

CONSTANCE: Isn't that what she told you?

MORTIMER: Yes.

CONSTANCE: It's quite easy to prove. If you won't take my word for it we can ring for the butler and you can ask him yourself. . . . Ring the bell, John, will you?

MORTIMER [*Uneasily*]: No, don't do that. If you give me your word, of course I must take it.

CONSTANCE: That's very kind of you. I'm grateful to you for not exposing me to the humiliation of making my butler corroborate my statement.

MORTIMER: If Marie-Louise was dining here why were you sitting on her bed?

CONSTANCE: John had to go out and do an operation, and Marie-Louise wanted to show me the things she'd got from Paris, so I walked round to your house. It was a lovely night. You remember that, don't you?

MORTIMER: Damn it, I've got more important things to do than look at the night.

CONSTANCE: We tried them all on and then we were rather tired, so Marie-Louise got into bed and I sat down and we talked.

MORTIMER: If you were tired why didn't you go home and go to bed?

CONSTANCE: John had promised to come round and fetch me.

MORTIMER: And did he? At what time did he come?

JOHN: I couldn't manage it. The operation took much longer than I expected. It was one of those cases where when you once start cutting you really don't know where to stop. You know the sort of thing, don't you, Mortimer?

MORTIMER: No, I don't. How the devil should I?

CONSTANCE: All that is neither here nor there. This is a

terrible accusation you've made against John and Marie-Louise and I'm very much upset. But I will remain perfectly calm till I've heard everything. Now let me have your proofs.

MORTIMER: My proofs? What d'you mean? The cigarette case. When I found the cigarette case I naturally put two and two together.

CONSTANCE [*With her eyes flashing*]: I quite understand, but why did you make them five?

MORTIMER [*Emphatically, in order not to show that he is wavering*]: It isn't possible that I should have made a mistake.

CONSTANCE: Even the richest of us may err. I remember when Mr. Pierpont Morgan died, he was found to own seven million dollars' of worthless securities.

MORTIMER [*Uneasily*]: You don't know what a shock it was, Constance. I had the most implicit confidence in Marie-Louise. I was knocked endways. I've been brooding over it ever since till I was afraid I should go mad.

CONSTANCE: And do you mean to say that you've come here and made a fearful scene just because you found my cigarette case in Marie-Louise's room? I can't believe it. You're a man of the world and a business man. You're extremely intelligent. Surely you have something to go upon. You must be holding something back. Don't be afraid of hurting my feelings. You've said so much now that I must insist on your saying everything. I want the truth and the whole truth.

[*There is a pause.* MORTIMER *looks from* MARIE-LOUISE, *who is quietly weeping, to* CONSTANCE, *with the utmost bewilderment.*]

MORTIMER: I'm afraid I've made a damned fool of myself.

CONSTANCE: I'm afraid you have.

MORTIMER: I'm awfully sorry, Constance. I beg your pardon.

CONSTANCE: Oh, don't bother about me. You've exposed me to the most bitter humiliation. You've sown seeds of distrust between me and John which can never be. . . .

[*She looks for a word.*]

MRS. CULVER [*Supplying it*]: Fertilized.

CONSTANCE [*Ignoring it*] : Uprooted. But I don't matter. It's Marie-Louise's pardon you must beg.

MORTIMER [*Humbly*] : Marie-Louise.

MARIE-LOUISE : Don't touch me. Don't come near me.

MORTIMER [*To* CONSTANCE, *miserably*] : You know what jealousy is.

CONSTANCE : Certainly not. I think it's a most ugly and despicable vice.

MORTIMER [*To* MARIE-LOUISE] : Marie-Louise, I'm sorry. Won't you forgive me?

MARIE-LOUISE : You've insulted me before all my friends. You know how devotedly I love Constance. You might have accused me of having an affair with any one else—but not John.

CONSTANCE : Not her greatest friend's husband. The milk-man or the dustman if you like, but not her greatest friend's husband.

MORTIMER : I've been a perfect swine. I don't know what came over me. I really wasn't responsible for my actions.

MARIE-LOUISE : I've loved you all these years. No one has ever loved you as I've loved you. Oh, it's cruel, cruel.

MORTIMER : Come away, darling. I can't say here what I want to say.

MARIE-LOUISE : No, no, no.

CONSTANCE [*Putting her hand on his arm, gently*] : I think you'd better leave her here for a little while, Morty. I'll talk to her when you've gone. She's naturally upset. A sensitive little thing like that.

MORTIMER : We're dining with the Vancouvers at 8.15.

CONSTANCE : For eight-thirty. I promise I'll send her home in good time to dress.

MORTIMER : She'll give me another chance?

CONSTANCE : Yes, yes.

MORTIMER : I'd do anything in the world for her. [CON-STANCE *puts her fingers to her lips and then points signifi-cantly to the pearl chain she is wearing. For a second* MORTI-MER *does not understand, but as soon as her notion dawns on him he gives a pleased nod*] You're the cleverest woman in the world. [*As he goes out he stops and holds out his hand to* JOHN] Will you shake hands with me, old man? I made a mistake and I'm man enough to acknowledge it.

JOHN [*Very cordially*]: Not at all, old boy. I quite agree that it did look fishy, the cigarette case. If I'd dreamt that Constance was going to leave an expensive thing like that lying about all over the place, I'm hanged if I'd have let her pinch it.

MORTIMER: You don't know what a weight it is off my mind. I felt a hundred when I came here, and now I feel like a two-year-old.

[*He goes out. The moment the door is closed behind him there is a general change in every attitude. The tension disappears and there is a feeling of relief.*]

JOHN: Constance, you're a brick. I shall never forget this. Never, so long as I live. And by George, what presence of mind you showed. I went hot and cold all over, and you never batted an eye-lash.

CONSTANCE: By the way, here is your cigarette case. You'd better have a ring made and hang it on your key-chain.

JOHN: No, no. Keep it. I'm too old to take these risks.

CONSTANCE: By the way, did any one see you go into Morty's house last night?

JOHN: No, we let ourselves in with Marie-Louise's latch key.

CONSTANCE: That's all right then. If Mortimer asks the servants they can tell him nothing. I had to take that chance.

MARIE-LOUISE [*With a little gesture of ashamed dismay*]: Oh, Constance, what must you think of me?

CONSTANCE: I? Exactly the same as I thought before. I think you're sweet, Marie-Louise.

MARIE-LOUISE: You have every right to be angry with me.

CONSTANCE: Perhaps, but not the inclination.

MARIE-LOUISE: Oh, it's not true. I've treated you shamefully. You've made me feel such a pig. And you had your chance to get back on me and you didn't take it. I'm so ashamed.

CONSTANCE [*Amused*]: Because you've been having an affair with John, or because you've been found out?

MARIE-LOUISE: Oh, Constance, don't be heartless. Say anything you like, curse me, stamp on me, but don't smile at me. I'm in a terrible position.

CONSTANCE: And you want me to make a scene. I know and I sympathize. [*Very calmly*] But the fact is that Mortimer told me nothing I didn't know before.

MARIE-LOUISE [*Aghast*]: Do you mean to say that you've known all along?

CONSTANCE: All along, darling. I've been spending the last six months in a desperate effort to prevent my friends and relations from telling me your ghastly secret. It's been very difficult sometimes. Often mother's profound understanding of life, Martha's passion for truth at any price, and Barbara's silent sympathy, have almost worn me down. But until to-day the t's were not definitely crossed nor the i's distinctly dotted, and I was able to ignore the facts that were staring at me—rather rudely, I must say—in the face.

MARIE-LOUISE: But why, why? It's not human. Why didn't you do anything?

CONSTANCE: That, darling, is my affair.

MARIE-LOUISE [*Thinking she understands*]: Oh, I see.

CONSTANCE [*Rather tartly*]: No, you don't. I have always been absolutely faithful to John. I have not winked at your intrigue in order to cover my own.

MARIE-LOUISE [*Beginning to be a little put out*]: I almost think you've been laughing at me up your sleeve all the time.

CONSTANCE [*Good-humouredly*]: Oh, my dear, you mustn't be offended just because I've taken away from you the satisfaction of thinking that you have been deceiving me all these months. I should hate you to think me capable of an intentional meanness.

MARIE-LOUISE: My head's going round and round.

CONSTANCE: Such a pretty head, too. Why don't you go and lie down? You want to look your best if you're dining with the Vancouvers.

MARIE-LOUISE: I wonder where Mortimer is?

CONSTANCE: You know that pearl necklace you showed me the other day and you said that Mortimer thought it cost a lot of money—well, he's gone to Cartier's to buy it for you.

MARIE-LOUISE [*Excitedly*] : Oh, Constance, do you think he has?

CONSTANCE : I think all men are born with the knowledge that when they have wounded a woman's soul—and our souls are easily wounded—the only cure is a trifling, but expensive, jewel.

MARIE-LOUISE : Do you think he'll have the sense to bring it home with him so that I can wear it to-night?

CONSTANCE : Oh, my dear, don't be such a fool as to accept it with alacrity. Remember that Mortimer has grievously insulted you, he's made the most shocking accusation that a man can make against his wife, he's trampled on your love and now he's destroyed your trust in him.

MARIE-LOUISE : Oh, how right you are, Constance.

CONSTANCE : Surely I need not tell you what to do. Refuse to speak to him, but never let him get a word of defense in edgeways. Cry enough to make him feel what a brute he is, but not enough to make your eyes swell. Say you'll leave him and run sobbing to the door, but take care to let him stop you before you open it. Repeat yourself. Say the same thing over and over again—it wears them down—and if he answers you take no notice, but just say it again. And at last when you've reduced him to desperation, when his head is aching as though it would split, when he's sweating at every pore, when he's harassed and miserable and haggard and broken—then consent as an unmerited favor, as a sign of your forgiving temper and the sweetness of your nature, to accept, no, don't consent, *deign* to accept the pearl necklace for which the wretch has just paid ten thousand pounds.

MARIE-LOUISE [*With peculiar satisfaction*] : Twelve, darling.

CONSTANCE : And don't thank him. That wouldn't be playing the game. Let him thank *you* for the favour you do him in allowing him to make you a paltry gift. Have you got your car here?

MARIE-LOUISE : No, I was in such a state when I came I took a taxi.

CONSTANCE : John, do take Marie-Louise down and put her in a taxi.

JOHN: All right.

MARIE-LOUISE: No, not John. I couldn't. After all, I have some delicacy.

CONSTANCE: Oh, have you? Well, let Bernard go.

BERNARD: I shall be pleased.

CONSTANCE [*To* BERNARD]: But come back, won't you?

BERNARD: Certainly.

MARIE-LOUISE [*Kissing* CONSTANCE]: This has been a lesson to me, darling. I'm not a fool, Constance. I can learn.

CONSTANCE: At least prudence, I hope.

[MARIE-LOUISE *goes out followed by* BERNARD KERSAL.]

JOHN: How did you guess that Marie-Louise had said she was dining here?

CONSTANCE: She's too crafty a woman to invent a new lie when an old one will serve.

JOHN: It would have been awkward if Mortimer had insisted on asking Bentley if it was true.

CONSTANCE: I knew he wouldn't dare. It's only if a man's a gentleman that he won't hesitate to do an ungentlemanly thing. Mortimer is on the boundary line and it makes him careful.

MARTHA [*Significantly*]: Don't you imagine your patients are growing a trifle restless, John?

JOHN: I like to keep them waiting. They grow more and more nervous as the minutes pass and when I recommend an operation that will cost them two hundred and fifty pounds they are too shaken to protest.

MARTHA [*Pursing her lips*]: I can't imagine you'll very much like to hear what I'm determined to say to Constance.

JOHN: It's because I shrewdly suspect that you have some very unpleasant things to say about me that I am prepared reluctantly to neglect the call of duty and listen to you with my own ears.

CONSTANCE: She's been exercising miracles of restraint for the last three months, John. I think she has a right to let herself go now.

JOHN: If she's suffering from suppressed desires she's

come to the wrong establishment. She ought to go to a psycho-analyst.

MARTHA: I've only got one thing to say, John, and I'm perfectly willing that you should hear it. [*To* CONSTANCE] I don't know what your reasons were for shielding that abominable woman. I can only suppose you wanted to avoid more scandal than was necessary. . . .

MRS. CULVER [*Interrupting*]: Before you go any further, my dear, you must let me put my word in. [*To* CONSTANCE] My dear child, I beg you not to decide anything in a hurry. We must all think things over. First of all you must listen to what John has to say for himself.

MARTHA: What can he have to say for himself?

CONSTANCE [*Ironically*]: What indeed?

JOHN: Not the right thing anyway. I've seen too much of married life. . . .

CONSTANCE [*Interrupting, with a smile*]: Let us be just. Other people's rather than your own.

JOHN [*Going on*]: To imagine that even the Archangel Gabriel could say the right thing.

CONSTANCE: I've no reason, however, to suppose that the Archangel Gabriel could ever find himself in such a predicament.

JOHN: I'm for it and I'm prepared to take what's coming to me.

CONSTANCE [*To the world in general*]: No man could say handsomer than that.

JOHN: I'm expecting you to make a scene, Constance. It's your right and your privilege. I'm willing to bear it. Give me hell. I deserve it. Drag me up and down the room by the hair of the head. Kick me in the face. Stamp on me. I'll grovel. I'll eat the dust. My name is mud. Mud.

CONSTANCE: My poor John, what is there to make a scene about?

JOHN: I know how badly I've treated you. I had a wife who was good, loving and faithful, devoted to my interests, a perfect mother and an excellent housekeeper. A woman ten times too good for me. If I'd had the smallest spark of de-

cency I couldn't have treated you like this. I haven't a word
to say for myself.

MARTHA [*Interrupting him*] : You've humiliated her to all
her friends.

JOHN : I've behaved neither like a gentleman nor a sports-
man.

MARTHA : Your conduct is inexcusable.

JOHN : I haven't a leg to stand on.

MARTHA : Even if you didn't love her, you might have
treated her with respect.

JOHN : I've been as heartless as a crocodile and as unscrupulous as a typhoid bacillus.

CONSTANCE : Between you, of course, you're leaving me
very little to say.

MARTHA : There *is* nothing to say. You're quite right. This
is the sort of occasion when it's beneath a woman's dignity
to make a scene. It just shows how little John knows women
to think that you could demean yourself to vulgar abuse.
[*To* JOHN] I suppose you'll have the decency to put no ob-
stacle in the way of Constance's getting her freedom.

MRS. CULVER : Oh, Constance, you're not going to divorce
him?

MARTHA : Mother, you're so weak. How can she go on
living with a man for whom she has no respect? What would
her life be with this creature whom she can only mistrust and
despise? Besides, you have to think of their child. How can
Constance allow her daughter to be contaminated by the
society of a person of this character?

CONSTANCE : John has always been an excellent father.
Let us give the devil his due.

MRS. CULVER : Don't be too hard, darling. I can understand that at the moment you feel bitter, but it would be very
sad if you let your bitterness warp your judgment.

CONSTANCE : I don't feel in the least bitter. I wish I looked
as sweet as I feel.

MRS. CULVER : You can't deceive a mother, my dear. I
know the angry resentment that you feel. Under the unfortunate circumstances it's only too natural.

CONSTANCE : When I look into my heart I can't find a

trace of resentment, except perhaps for John's being so stupid as to let himself be found out.

JOHN: Let me say this in justification for myself, Constance. I did my little best to prevent it. Angels could do no more.

CONSTANCE: And angels presumably have not the pernicious habit of smoking straight-cut cigarettes.

JOHN: When you once get the taste for them, you prefer them to gippies.

MRS. CULVER: Don't be cynical, darling. That is the worst way to ease an aching heart. Come to your mother's arms, my dear, and let us have a good cry together. And then you'll feel better.

CONSTANCE: It's sweet of you, mother, but honestly I couldn't squeeze a tear out of my eyes if my life depended on it.

MRS. CULVER: And don't be too hard. Of course John is to blame. I admit that. He's been very, very naughty. But men are weak and women are so unscrupulous. I'm sure he's sorry for all the pain he's caused you.

MARTHA: What puzzles me is that you didn't do something the moment you discovered that John was having an affair.

CONSTANCE: To tell you the truth, I thought it no business of mine.

MARTHA [Indignantly]: Aren't you his wife?

CONSTANCE: John and I are very lucky people. Our marriage has been ideal.

MARTHA: How can you say that?

CONSTANCE: For five years we adored each other. That's much longer than most people do. Our honeymoon lasted five years and then we had a most extraordinary stroke of luck: we ceased to be in love with one another simultaneously.

JOHN: I protest, Constance. I've never ceased to be absolutely devoted to you.

CONSTANCE: I never said you had, darling. I'm convinced of it. I've never ceased to be devoted to you. We've shared one another's interests, we've loved to be together, I've

exulted in your success and you've trembled in my illness.
We've laughed at the same jokes and sighed over the same
worries. I don't know any couple that's been bound together
by a more genuine affection. But honestly, for the last ten
years have you been in love with me?

JOHN: You can't expect a man who's been married for fifteen years. . . .

CONSTANCE: My dear, I'm not asking for excuses. I'm
only asking for a plain answer.

JOHN: In the long run I enjoy your society much more
than anybody else's. There's no one I like so much as you.
You're the prettiest woman I've ever known and I shall say
the same when you're a hundred.

CONSTANCE: But does your heart leap into your mouth
when you hear my footstep on the stairs, and when I come
into the room, is your first impulse to catch me in your manly
arms? I haven't noticed it.

JOHN: I don't want to make a fool of myself.

CONSTANCE: Then I think you've answered my question.
You're no more in love with me than I am with you.

JOHN: You never said a word of this before.

CONSTANCE: I think most married couples tell one another far too much. There are some things that two people
may know very well, but which it's much more tactful for
them to pretend they don't.

JOHN: How did you find out?

CONSTANCE: I'll tell you. One night as we were dancing together, all at once I noticed that we weren't keeping such
good step as we generally did. It was because my mind was
wandering. I was thinking how it would suit me to do my
hair like a woman who was dancing alongside of us. Then I
looked at you and I saw you were thinking what pretty legs
she'd got. I suddenly realized that you weren't in love with
me any more and at the same moment I realized that it was
a relief, because I wasn't in love with you.

JOHN: I must say it never occurred to me for a moment.

CONSTANCE: I know. A man thinks it quite natural that
he should fall out of love with a woman, but it never strikes
him for a moment that a woman can do anything so unnat-

ural as to fall out of love with him. Don't be upset at that, darling, that is one of the charming limitations of your sex.

MARTHA: Do you mean mother and me to understand that since then John has been having one affair after another and you haven't turned a hair?

CONSTANCE: Since this is the first time he's been found out, let us give him the benefit of the doubt and hope that till now he has never strayed from the strict and narrow path. You're not angry with me, John?

JOHN: No, darling, not angry. But I *am* a little taken aback. I think you've been making rather a damned fool of me. It never struck me that your feelings for me had changed so much. You can't expect me to like it.

CONSTANCE: Oh, come now, you must be reasonable. You surely wouldn't wish me to have languished for all these years in a hopeless passion for you when you had nothing to give me in return but friendship and affection. Think what a bore it is to have some one in love with you whom you're not in love with.

JOHN: I can't conceive of your ever being a bore, Constance.

CONSTANCE [*Kissing her hand to him*]: Don't you realize that we must thank our lucky stars? We are the favoured of the gods. I shall never forget those five years of exquisite happiness you gave me when I loved you, and I shall never cease to be grateful to you, not because you loved me, but because you inspired me with love. Our love never degenerated into weariness. Because we ceased loving one another at the very same moment we never had to put up with quarrels and reproaches, recriminations and all the other paraphernalia of a passion that has ceased on one side and is still alive and eager on the other. Our love was like a cross-word puzzle in which we both hit upon the last word at the same moment. That is why our lives since have been so happy; that is why ours is a perfect marriage.

MARTHA: Do you mean to say that it meant nothing to you when you found out that John was carrying on with Marie-Louise?

CONSTANCE: Human nature is very imperfect. I'm afraid

I must admit that at the first moment I was vexed. But only at the first moment. Then I reflected that it was most unreasonable to be angry with John for giving to another something that I had no use for. That would be too much like a dog in the manger. And then I was fond enough of John to be willing that he should be happy in his own way. And if he was going to indulge in an intrigue . . . isn't that the proper phrase, John?

JOHN: I have not yet made up my mind whether it really is an indulgence.

CONSTANCE: Then it was much better that the object of his affections should be so intimate a friend of mine that I could keep a maternal eye on him.

JOHN: Really, Constance.

CONSTANCE: Marie-Louise is very pretty so that my self-esteem was not offended, and so rich that it was certain John would have no reason to squander money on her to the inconvenience of myself. She's not clever enough to acquire any ascendency over him, and so long as I kept his heart I was quite willing that she should have his senses. If you wanted to deceive me, John, I couldn't have chosen any one with whom I would more willingly be deceived than Marie-Louise.

JOHN: I don't gather that you have been very grossly deceived, darling. You have such penetration that when you look at me I feel as though I were shivering without a stitch of clothing on.

MRS. CULVER: I don't approve of your attitude, Constance. In my day when a young wife discovered that her husband had been deceiving her, she burst into a flood of tears and went to stay with her mother for three weeks, not returning to her husband till he had been brought to a proper state of abjection and repentance.

MARTHA: Are we to understand then that you are not going to divorce John?

CONSTANCE: You know, I can never see why a woman should give up a comfortable home, a considerable part of her income and the advantage of having a man about to do all the tiresome and disagreeable things for her, because he has been unfaithful to her. She's merely cutting off her nose to spite her face.

MARTHA: I am at a loss for words. I cannot conceive how a woman of any spirit can sit down and allow her husband to make a perfect damned fool of her.

CONSTANCE: You've been very stupid, my poor John. In the ordinary affairs of life stupidity is much more tiresome than wickedness. You can mend the vicious, but what in Heaven's name are you to do with the foolish?

JOHN: I've been a fool, Constance. I know it, but I'm capable of learning by experience, so I can't be a damned fool.

CONSTANCE: You mean that in the future you'll be more careful to cover your tracks?

MRS. CULVER: Oh, no, Constance, he means that this has been a lesson to him, and that in the future you'll have no cause for complaint.

CONSTANCE: I've always been given to understand that men only abandon their vices when advancing years have made them a burden rather than a pleasure. John, I'm happy to say, is still in the flower of his age. I suppose you give yourself another fifteen years, John, don't you?

JOHN: Really, Constance, I don't know what you mean. The things you say sometimes are positively embarrassing.

CONSTANCE: I think at all events we may take it that Marie-Louise will have more than one successor.

JOHN: Constance, I give you my word of honour. . . .

CONSTANCE [*Interrupting*]: That is the only gift you can make for which I can find no use. You see, so long as I was able to pretend a blissful ignorance of your goings-on we could all be perfectly happy. You were enjoying yourself and I received a lot of sympathy as the outraged wife. But now I do see that the position is very difficult. You have put me in a position that is neither elegant nor dignified.

JOHN: I'm awfully sorry, Constance.

MARTHA: You're going to leave him?

CONSTANCE: No, I'm not going to leave him. John, you remember that Barbara offered to take me into her business?

I refused. Well, I've changed my mind and I'm going to accept.

JOHN: But why? I don't see your point.

CONSTANCE: I'm not prepared any more to be entirely dependent upon you, John.

JOHN: But, my dear, everything I earn is at your disposal. It's a pleasure for me to provide for your wants. Heaven knows, they're not very great.

CONSTANCE: I know. Come, John, I've been very reasonable, haven't I? Don't try and thwart me when I want to do something on which I've set my heart.

[*There is an instant's pause.*]

JOHN: I don't understand. But if you put it like that, I haven't a word to say. Of course, you must do exactly as you wish.

CONSTANCE: That's a dear. Now go back to your patients or else I shall have to keep you as well as myself.

JOHN: Will you give me a kiss?

CONSTANCE: Why not?

JOHN [*Kissing her*]: It's peace between us?

CONSTANCE: Peace and good-will. [JOHN *goes out*] He is rather sweet, isn't he?

MRS. CULVER: What have you got on your mind, Constance?

CONSTANCE: I, mother? [*Teasing her*] What do you suspect?

MRS. CULVER: I don't like the look of you.

CONSTANCE: I'm sorry for that. Most people find me far from plain.

MRS. CULVER: You've got some deviltry in mind, but for the life of me I can't guess it.

MARTHA: I can't see what you expect to get out of working with Barbara.

CONSTANCE: Between a thousand and fifteen hundred a year, I believe.

MARTHA: I wasn't thinking of the money, and you know it.

CONSTANCE: I'm tired of being the modern wife.

MARTHA: What do you mean by the modern wife?

CONSTANCE: A prostitute who doesn't deliver the goods.

MRS. CULVER: My dear, what would your father say if he heard you say such things?

CONSTANCE: Darling, need we conjecture the remarks of a gentleman who's been dead for five and twenty years? Had he any gift for repartee?

MRS. CULVER: None whatever. He was good, but he was stupid. That is why the gods loved him and he died young.

[BERNARD KERSAL *opens the door and looks in.*]

BERNARD: May I come in?

CONSTANCE: Oh, there you are. I wondered what had become of you.

BERNARD: When Marie-Louise saw my two-seater at the door she asked me to drive her. I couldn't very well refuse.

CONSTANCE: So you took her home.

BERNARD: No, she said she was in such a state she must have her hair washed. I drove her to a place in Bond Street.

CONSTANCE: And what did she say to you?

BERNARD: She said, "I don't know what you must think of me."

CONSTANCE: That is what most women say to a man when his opinion doesn't matter two straws to them. And what did you answer?

BERNARD: Well, I said, "I prefer not to offer an opinion on a matter which is no business of mine."

CONSTANCE: Dear Bernard, one of the things I like most in you is that you always remain so perfectly in character. If the heavens fell you would still remain the perfect English gentleman.

BERNARD: I thought it the most tactful thing to say.

CONSTANCE: Well, mother, I won't detain you any longer. I know that you and Martha have a thousand things to do.

MRS. CULVER: I'm glad you reminded me. Come, Martha. Good-bye, darling. Good-bye, Mr. Kersal.

BERNARD: Good-bye.

CONSTANCE [*To* MARTHA]: Good-bye, dear. Thank you for all your sympathy. You've been a great help in my hour of need.

MARTHA: I don't understand and it's no good saying I do.

CONSTANCE: Bless you. [MRS. CULVER *and* MARTHA *go*

out. BERNARD *closes the door after them*] Shall we be very late?

BERNARD: So late that it doesn't matter if we're a little later. I have something important to say to you.

CONSTANCE [*Teasing him a little*]: Important to me or important to you?

BERNARD: I can't tell you how distressed I was at that terrible scene.

CONSTANCE: Oh, didn't you think it had its lighter moments?

BERNARD: It's only this afternoon I learned the truth, and then I never imagined for a moment that you knew it too. I can't tell you how brave I think it of you to have borne all this torture with a smiling face. If I admired you before, I admire you ten times more now.

CONSTANCE: You're very sweet, Bernard.

BERNARD: My heart bleeds when I think of what you've gone through.

CONSTANCE: It's not a very good plan to take other people's misfortunes too much to heart.

BERNARD: Hardly an hour ago I told you that if ever you wanted me I was only too anxious to do anything in the world for you. I little thought then that the time would come so soon. There's no reason now why I shouldn't tell you of the love that consumes me. Oh, Constance, come to me. You know that if things were as I thought they were between you and John nothing would have induced me to say a word. But now he has no longer any claims on you. He doesn't love you. Why should you go on wasting your life with a man who is capable of exposing you to all this humiliation? You know how long and tenderly I've loved you. You can trust yourself to me. I'll give my whole life to making you forget the anguish you've endured. Will you marry me, Constance?

CONSTANCE: My dear, John may have behaved very badly but he's still my husband.

BERNARD: Only in name. You've done everything in your power to save a scandal and now if you ask him to let himself be divorced he's bound to consent.

CONSTANCE: Do you really think John has behaved so very badly to me?

BERNARD [*Astonished*]: You don't mean to say that you have any doubts in your mind about his relationship with Marie-Louise?

CONSTANCE: None.

BERNARD: Then what in God's name do you mean?

CONSTANCE: My dear Bernard, have you ever considered what marriage is among well-to-do people? In the working classes a woman cooks her husband's dinner, washes for him and darns his socks. She looks after the children and makes their clothes. She gives good value for the money she costs. But what is a wife in our class? Her house is managed by servants, nurses look after her children, if she has resigned herself to having any, and as soon as they are old enough she packs them off to school. Let us face it, she is no more than the mistress of a man of whose desire she has taken advantage to insist on a legal ceremony that will prevent him from discarding her when his desire has ceased.

BERNARD: She's also his companion and his helpmate.

CONSTANCE: My dear, any sensible man would sooner play bridge at his club than with his wife, and he'd always rather play golf with a man than with a woman. A paid secretary is a far better helpmate than a loving spouse. When all is said and done, the modern wife is nothing but a parasite.

BERNARD: I don't agree with you.

CONSTANCE: You see, my poor friend, you are in love and your judgment is confused.

BERNARD: I don't understand what you mean.

CONSTANCE: John gives me board and lodging, money for my clothes and my amusements, a car to drive in and a certain position in the world. He's bound to do all that because fifteen years ago he was madly in love with me, and he undertook it; though, if you'd asked him, he would certainly have acknowledged that nothing is so fleeting as that particular form of madness called love. It was either very generous of him or very imprudent. Don't you think it would be rather shabby of me to take advantage now of his generosity or his want of foresight?

BERNARD: In what way?

CONSTANCE: He paid a very high price for something that he couldn't get cheaper. He no longer wants that. Why should I resent it? I know as well as anybody else that desire is fleeting. It comes and goes and no man can understand why. The only thing that's certain is that when it's gone it's gone forever. So long as John continues to provide for me what right have I to complain that he is unfaithful to me? He bought a toy and if he no longer wants to play with it why should he? He paid for it.

BERNARD: That might be all right if a man had only to think about himself. What about the woman?

CONSTANCE: I don't think you need waste too much sympathy on her. Like ninety-nine girls out of a hundred when I married I looked upon it as the only easy, honourable and lucrative calling open to me. When the average woman who has been married for fifteen years discovers her husband's infidelity it is not her heart that is wounded but her vanity. If she had any sense, she would regard it merely as one of the necessary inconveniences of an otherwise pleasant profession.

BERNARD: Then the long and short of it is that you don't love me.

CONSTANCE: You think that my principles are all moonshine?

BERNARD: I don't think they would have much influence if you were as crazy about me as I am about you. Do you still love John?

CONSTANCE: I'm very fond of him, he makes me laugh, and we get on together like a house on fire, but I'm not in love with him.

BERNARD: And is that enough for you? Isn't the future sometimes a trifle desolate? Don't you want love?

[*A pause. She gives him a long reflective look.*]

CONSTANCE [*Charmingly*]: If I did I should come to you for it, Bernard.

BERNARD: Constance, what do you mean? Is it possible

that you could ever care for me? Oh, my darling, I worship the ground you tread on.

[*He seizes her in his arms and kisses her passionately.*]

CONSTANCE [*Releasing herself*]: Oh, my dear, don't be so sudden. I should despise myself entirely if I were unfaithful to John so long as I am entirely dependent on him.

BERNARD: But if you love me?

CONSTANCE: I never said I did. But even if I did, so long as John provides me with all the necessities of existence I wouldn't be unfaithful. It all comes down to the economic situation. He has bought my fidelity and I should be worse than a harlot if I took the price he paid and did not deliver the goods.

BERNARD: Do you mean to say there's no hope for me at all?

CONSTANCE: The only hope before you at the moment is to start for Ranelagh before the game is over.

BERNARD: Do you still want to go?

CONSTANCE: Yes.

BERNARD: Very well. [*With a burst of passion*] I love you.

CONSTANCE: Then go down and start up the car, put a spot of oil in the radiator or something, and I'll join you in a minute. I want to telephone.

BERNARD: Very well.

[*He goes out.* CONSTANCE *takes up the telephone.*]

CONSTANCE: Mayfair 2646. . . . Barbara? It's Constance. That offer you made me a fortnight ago—is it still open? Well, I want to accept it. . . . No, no, nothing has happened. John is very well. He's always sweet, you know. It's only that I want to earn my own living. When can I start? The sooner the better.

THE END OF ACT TWO

ACT THREE

*The scene is the same as in the preceding acts. A year has
passed. It is afternoon.*

CONSTANCE is seated at a desk writing letters. THE
BUTLER *shows in* BARBARA FAWCETT *and* MARTHA.

BENTLEY: Mrs. Fawcett and Miss Culver.

CONSTANCE: Oh! Sit down, I'm just finishing a note.

BARBARA: We met on the doorstep.

MARTHA: I thought I'd just look round and see if there
was anything I could do to help you before you start.

CONSTANCE: That's very nice of you, Martha. I really
don't think there is. I'm packed and ready, and for once I
don't believe I've forgotten one of the things I shan't want.

BARBARA: I felt I must run in to say good-bye to you.

CONSTANCE: Now, my dear, you mustn't neglect your
work the moment my back is turned.

BARBARA: Well, it's partly the work that's brought me.
An order has just come in for a new house and they want an
Italian room.

CONSTANCE: I don't like that look in your beady eye,
Barbara.

BARBARA: Well, it struck me that as you're going to Italy
you might go round the shops and buy any nice pieces that
you can find.

CONSTANCE: Perish the thought. I've worked like a dog
for a year and last night at six o'clock I downed tools. I
stripped off my grimy overalls, wrung the sweat from my
honest brow and scrubbed my horny hands. You said I could
take six weeks' holiday.

BARBARA: I admit that you've thoroughly earned it.

CONSTANCE: When I closed the shop-door behind me, I
ceased to be a British workingman and resumed the position
of a perfect English lady.

MARTHA: I never saw you in such spirits.

CONSTANCE: Something accomplished, something done.
But what I was coming to was this: for the next six weeks I

refuse to give a moment's thought to bathrooms or wall-papers, kitchen sinks, scullery floors, curtains, cushions and refrigerators.

BARBARA: I wasn't asking you to. I only wanted you to get some of that painted Italian furniture and a few mirrors.

CONSTANCE: No, I've worked hard and I've enjoyed my work, and now I'm going to enjoy a perfect holiday.

BARBARA: Oh, well, have it your own way.

MARTHA: Constance dear, I think there's something you ought to know.

CONSTANCE: I should have thought you had discovered by now that I generally know the things I ought to know.

MARTHA: You'll never guess whom I saw in Bond Street this morning.

CONSTANCE: Yes, I shall. Marie-Louise.

MARTHA: Oh!

CONSTANCE: I'm sorry to disappoint you, darling. She rang me up an hour ago.

MARTHA: But I thought she wasn't coming back for an-other month. She was going to stay away a year.

CONSTANCE: She arrived last night and I'm expecting her every minute.

MARTHA: Here?

CONSTANCE: Yes. She said she simply must run in and see me before I left.

MARTHA: I wonder what she wants.

CONSTANCE: Perhaps to pass the time of day. I think it's rather sweet of her, considering how busy she must be on getting back after so long.

BARBARA: She's been all over the place, hasn't she?

CONSTANCE: Yes, she's been in Malaya; Mortimer has in-terests there, you know, and in China, and now they've just come from India.

MARTHA: I often wondered if it was at your suggestion that they set off on that long tour immediately after that unfortunate scene.

CONSTANCE: Which, you must confess, no one enjoyed more than you, darling.

BARBARA: It was certainly the most sensible thing they could do.

MARTHA: Of course you know your own business best, darling, but don't you think it's a little unfortunate that you should be going away for six weeks just as she comes back?

CONSTANCE: We workingwomen have to take our holidays when we can.

BARBARA: Surely John has had his lesson. He's not going to make a fool of himself a second time.

MARTHA: Do you think he has really got over his infatuation, Constance?

CONSTANCE: I don't know at all. But here he is, you'd better ask him.

[*As she says these words,* JOHN *enters.*]

JOHN: Ask him what?

MARTHA [*Not at all at a loss*]: I was just wondering what you'd do with yourself during Constance's absence.

JOHN: I've got a lot of work, you know, and I shall go to the club a good deal.

MARTHA: It seems a pity that you weren't able to arrange things so that you and Constance should take your holidays together.

BARBARA: Don't blame me for that. I was quite willing to make my arrangements to suit Constance.

CONSTANCE: You see, I wanted to go to Italy and the only places John likes on the Continent are those in which it's only by an effort of the imagination that you can tell you're not in England.

MARTHA: What about Helen?

CONSTANCE: We've taken a house at Henley for August. John can play golf and go on the river and I shall be able to come up to town every day to look after the business.

BARBARA: Well, dear, I'll leave you. I hope you'll have a wonderful holiday. I know you've deserved it. Do you know, I think I'm a very clever woman, John, to have persuaded Constance to work. She's been absolutely invaluable to me.

JOHN: I never liked the idea and I'm not going to say I did.

BARBARA: Haven't you forgiven me yet?

JOHN: She insisted on it and I had to make the best of a bad job.

BARBARA: Good-bye.

CONSTANCE [*Kissing her*]: Good-bye, dear. Take care of yourself.

MARTHA: I'll come with you, Barbara. Mother said she'd look in for a minute to say good-bye to you.

CONSTANCE: Oh, all right. Good-bye.

[*She kisses the two and accompanies them to the door. They go out.*]

JOHN: I say, Constance, I thought you had to go now because Barbara couldn't possibly get away.

CONSTANCE: Did I say that?

JOHN: Certainly.

CONSTANCE: Oh!

JOHN: If I'd dreamt that you could just as easily take your holiday when I take mine. . . .

CONSTANCE [*Interrupting*]: Don't you think it's a mistake for husbands and wives to take their holidays together? The only reason one takes a holiday is for rest and change and recreation. Do you think a man really gets that when he goes away with his wife?

JOHN: It depends on the wife.

CONSTANCE: I know nothing more depressing than the sight of all those couples in a hotel dining room, one little couple to one little table, sitting opposite to one another without a word to say.

JOHN: Oh, nonsense. You often see couples who are very jolly and cheerful.

CONSTANCE: Yes, I know, but look closely at the lady's wedding-ring and you'll see that it rests uneasily on the hand it adorns.

JOHN: We always get on like a house on fire and when I slipped a wedding-ring on your finger a bishop supervised the process. You're not going to tell me that I bore *you*.

CONSTANCE: On the contrary, you tickle me to death. It's that unhappy modesty of mine: I was afraid that you could have too much of my society. I thought it would refresh you if I left you to your own devices for a few weeks.

JOHN: If you go on pulling my leg so persistently I shall be permanently deformed.

CONSTANCE: Anyhow it's too late now. My bags are packed, my farewells made and nothing bores people so much as to see you to-morrow when they've made up their minds to get on without you for a month.

JOHN: H'm. Eyewash. . . . Look here, Constance, there's something I want to say to you.

CONSTANCE: Yes?

JOHN: Do you know that Marie-Louise has come back?

CONSTANCE: Yes. She said she'd try and look in to say how do you do before I started. It'll be nice to see her again after so long.

JOHN: I want you to do something for me, Constance.

CONSTANCE: What is it?

JOHN: Well, you've been a perfect brick to me, and hang it all, I can't take advantage of your good nature. I must do the square thing.

CONSTANCE: I'm afraid I don't quite understand.

JOHN: I haven't seen Marie-Louise since that day when Mortimer came here and made such a fool of himself. She's been away for nearly a year and taking all things into consideration I think it would be a mistake to resume the relations that we were on then.

CONSTANCE: What makes you think she wishes to?

JOHN: The fact that she rang you up the moment she arrived looks ominous to me.

CONSTANCE: Ominous? You know some women can't see a telephone without taking the receiver off and then, when the operator says, "Number, please," they have to say something. I dare say ours was the first that occurred to Marie-Louise.

JOHN: It's no good blinking the fact that Marie-Louise was madly in love with me.

CONSTANCE: Well, we can neither of us blame her for that.

JOHN: I don't want to be unkind, but after all, circumstances have forced a break upon us and I think we had better look upon it as permanent.

CONSTANCE: Of course you must please yourself.

JOHN: I'm not thinking of myself, Constance. I'm thinking partly of course of Marie-Louise's good, but, I confess, chiefly of you. I could never look you in the face again if everything between Marie-Louise and me were not definitely finished.

CONSTANCE: I should hate you to lose so harmless and inexpensive a pleasure.

JOHN: Of course it'll be painful, but if one's made up one's mind to do a thing I think it's much better to do it quickly.

CONSTANCE: I think you're quite right. I'll tell you what I'll do, as soon as Marie-Louise comes I'll make an excuse and leave you alone with her.

JOHN: That wasn't exactly my idea.

CONSTANCE: Oh?

JOHN: It's the kind of thing that a woman can do so much better than a man. It struck me that it would come better from you than from me.

CONSTANCE: Oh, did it?

JOHN: It's a little awkward for me, but it would be quite easy for you to say—well, you know the sort of thing, that you have your self-respect to think of, and to cut a long story short, she must either give me up or you'll raise hell.

CONSTANCE: But you know what a soft heart I have. If she bursts into tears and says she can't live without you I shall feel so sorry for her that I shall say, "Well, damn it all, keep him."

JOHN: You wouldn't do me a dirty trick like that, Constance.

CONSTANCE: You know that your happiness is my chief interest in life.

JOHN [*After a moment's hesitation*]: Constance, I will be perfectly frank with you. I'm fed up with Marie-Louise.

CONSTANCE: Darling, why didn't you say that at once?

JOHN: Be a sport, Constance. You know that's not the kind of thing one can say to a woman.

CONSTANCE: I admit it's not the kind of thing she's apt to take very well.

JOHN: Women are funny. When they're tired of you they tell you so without a moment's hesitation and if you don't like it you can lump it. But if you're tired of them you're a brute and a beast and boiling oil's too good for you.

CONSTANCE: Very well, leave it to me. I'll do it.

JOHN: You're a perfect brick. But you'll let her down gently, won't you? I wouldn't hurt her feelings for the world. She's a nice little thing, Constance.

CONSTANCE: Sweet.

JOHN: And it's hard luck on her.

CONSTANCE: Rotten.

JOHN: Make her understand that I'm more sinned against than sinning. I don't want her to think too badly of me.

CONSTANCE: Of course not.

JOHN: But be quite sure it's definite.

CONSTANCE: Leave it to me.

JOHN: You're a ripper, Constance. By George, no man could want a better wife.

[*The butler introduces* MARIE-LOUISE.]

BUTLER: Mrs. Durham.

[*The two women embrace warmly.*]

MARIE-LOUISE: Darling, how perfectly divine to see you again. It's too, too wonderful.

CONSTANCE: My dear, how well you're looking. Are those the new pearls?

MARIE-LOUISE: Aren't they sweet? But Mortimer bought me the most heavenly emeralds when we were in India. Oh, John, how are you?

JOHN: Oh, I'm all right, thanks.

MARIE-LOUISE: Aren't you a little fatter than when I saw you last?

JOHN: Certainly not.

MARIE-LOUISE: I've lost pounds. [*To* CONSTANCE] I'm so glad I caught you. I should have been so disappointed to miss you. [*To* JOHN] Where are you going?

JOHN: Nowhere. Constance is going alone.

MARIE-LOUISE: Is she? How perfectly divine. I suppose you can't get away. Are you making pots of money?

JOHN: I get along. Will you forgive me if I leave you? I've got to be off.

MARIE-LOUISE: Of course. You're always busy, aren't you?

JOHN: Good-bye.

MARIE-LOUISE: I hope we shall see something of you while Constance is away.

JOHN: Thank you very much.

MARIE-LOUISE: Mortimer's golf has improved. He'd love to play with you.

JOHN: Oh, yes, I should love it.

[*He goes out.*]

MARIE-LOUISE: I did so hope to find you alone. Constance, I've got heaps and heaps to tell you. Isn't it tactful of John to leave us? First of all I want to tell you how splendidly everything has turned out. You know you were quite right. I'm so glad I took your advice and made Mortimer take me away for a year.

CONSTANCE: Mortimer is no fool.

MARIE-LOUISE: Oh, no, for a man he's really quite clever. I gave him hell, you know, for ever having suspected me, and at last he was just eating out of my hand. But I could see he wasn't quite sure of me. You know what men are— when they once get an idea in their heads it's dreadfully difficult for them to get it out again. But the journey was an inspiration; I was absolutely angelic all the time, and he made a lot of money, so everything in the garden was rosy.

CONSTANCE: I'm very glad.

MARIE-LOUISE: I owe it all to you, Constance. I made Mortimer buy you a perfectly divine star sapphire in Ceylon. I told him he owed you some sort of reparation for the insult he'd put upon you. It cost a hundred and twenty pounds, darling, and we're taking it to Cartier's to have it set.

CONSTANCE: How thrilling.

MARIE-LOUISE: You mustn't think I'm ungrateful. Now listen, Constance, I want to tell you at once that you needn't distress yourself about me and John.

CONSTANCE: I never did.

MARIE-LOUISE: I know I behaved like a little beast, but I never thought you'd find out. If I had, well, you know me well enough to be positive that nothing would have induced me to have anything to do with him.

CONSTANCE: You're very kind.

MARIE-LOUISE: I want you to do something for me, Constance. Will you?

CONSTANCE: I'm always eager to oblige a friend.

MARIE-LOUISE: Well, you know what John is. Of course he's a dear and all that kind of thing, but the thing's over and it's best that he should realize it at once.

CONSTANCE: Over?

MARIE-LOUISE: Of course I know he's head over heels in love with me still. I saw that the moment I came into the room. One can't blame him for that, can one?

CONSTANCE: Men do find you fascinating.

MARIE-LOUISE: But one has to think of oneself sometimes in this world. He must see that it could never be the same after we discovered that you knew all about it.

CONSTANCE: I kept it from you as long as I could.

MARIE-LOUISE: One couldn't help feeling then that you were rather making fools of us. It seemed to take the romance away if you see what I mean.

CONSTANCE: Dimly.

MARIE-LOUISE: You know, I wouldn't hurt John's feelings for the world, but it's no good beating around the bush and I'm quite determined to have the thing finished and done with before you go.

CONSTANCE: This is very sudden. I'm afraid it'll be an awful shock to John.

MARIE-LOUISE: I've quite made up my mind.

CONSTANCE: There isn't much time for a very long and moving scene, but I'll see if John is in still. Could you manage it in ten minutes?

MARIE-LOUISE: Oh, but *I* can't see him. I want you to tell him.

CONSTANCE: Me!

MARIE-LOUISE: You know him so well, you know just the sort of things to say to him. It's not very nice telling a man who adores you that you don't care for him in that way any more. It's so much easier for a third party.

CONSTANCE: Do you really think so?

MARIE-LOUISE: I'm positive of it. You see, you can say that for your sake I've made up my mind that from now on we can be nothing but friends. You've been so wonderful to both of us, it would be dreadful if we didn't play the game now. Say that I shall always think of him tenderly and that he's the only man I've ever really loved, but that we must part.

CONSTANCE: But if he insists on seeing you?

MARIE-LOUISE: It's no good, Constance, I can't see him. I shall only cry and get my eyes all bunged up. You will do it for me, darling. Please.

CONSTANCE: I will.

MARIE-LOUISE: I got the most divine evening frock in pale green satin on my way through Paris and it would look too sweet on you. Would you like me to give it to you? I've only worn it once.

CONSTANCE: Now tell me the real reason why you're so determined to get rid of John without a moment's delay.

[MARIE-LOUISE *looks at her and gives a little roguish smile.*]

MARIE-LOUISE: Swear you won't tell.

CONSTANCE: On my honour.

MARIE-LOUISE: Well, my dear, we met a perfectly divine young man in India. He was A.D.C. to one of the governors and he came home on the same boat with us. He simply adores me.

CONSTANCE: And of course you adore him.

MARIE-LOUISE: My dear, I'm absolutely mad about him. I don't know what's going to happen.

CONSTANCE: I think we can both give a pretty shrewd guess.

MARIE-LOUISE: It's simply awful to have a temperament like mine. Of course you can't understand, you're cold.

CONSTANCE [*Very calmly*]: You're an immoral little beast, Marie-Louise.

MARIE-LOUISE: Oh, I'm not. I have affairs—but I'm not promiscuous.

CONSTANCE: I should respect you more if you were an

honest prostitute. She at least does what she does to earn her bread and butter. You take everything from your husband and give him nothing that he pays for. You are no better than a vulgar cheat.

MARIE-LOUISE [*Surprised and really hurt*]: Constance, how can you say such things to me? I think it's terribly unkind of you. I thought you liked me.

CONSTANCE: I do. I think you a liar, a humbug and a parasite, but I like you.

MARIE-LOUISE: You can't if you think such dreadful things about me.

CONSTANCE: I do. You're good-tempered and generous and sometimes amusing. I even have a certain affection for you.

MARIE-LOUISE [*Smiling*]: I don't believe you mean a word you say. You know how devoted I am to you.

CONSTANCE: I take people as they are and I dare say that in another twenty years you'll be the pink of propriety.

MARIE-LOUISE: Darling, I knew you didn't mean it, but you will have your little joke.

CONSTANCE: Now run along, darling, and I'll break the news to John.

MARIE-LOUISE: Well, good-bye, and be gentle with him. There is no reason why we shouldn't spare him as much as possible. [*She turns to go and at the door—stops*] Of course I've often wondered why with your looks you don't have more success than you do. I know now.

CONSTANCE: Tell me.

MARIE-LOUISE: You see—you're a humourist and that always puts men off. [*She goes out. In a moment the door is cautiously opened and* JOHN *puts his head in*]

JOHN: Has she gone?

CONSTANCE: Come in. A fine night and all's well.

JOHN [*Entering*]: I heard the door bang. You broke it to her?

CONSTANCE: I broke it.

JOHN: Was she awfully upset?

CONSTANCE: Of course it was a shock, but she kept a stiff upper lip.

JOHN: Did she cry?

CONSTANCE: No. Not exactly. To tell you the truth I think she was stunned by the blow. But of course when she gets home and realises the full extent of her loss, she'll cry like anything.

JOHN: I hate to see a woman cry.

CONSTANCE: It is painful, isn't it? But of course it's a relief to the nerves.

JOHN: I think you're rather cool about it, Constance. I am not feeling any too comfortable. I shouldn't like her to think I'd treated her badly.

CONSTANCE: I think she quite understands that you're doing it for my sake. She knows that you have still a very great regard for her.

JOHN: But you made it quite definite, didn't you?

CONSTANCE: Oh, quite.

JOHN: I'm really very much obliged to you, Constance.

CONSTANCE: Not at all.

JOHN: At all events I'm glad to think that you'll be able to set out on your holiday with a perfectly easy mind. By the way, do you want any money? I'll write you a cheque at once.

CONSTANCE: Oh, no, thank you. I've got plenty. I've earned fourteen hundred pounds during this year that I've been working.

JOHN: Have you, by Jove! That's a very considerable sum.

CONSTANCE: I'm taking two hundred of it for my holiday. I've spent two hundred on my clothes and on odds and ends and the remaining thousand I've paid into your account this morning for my board and lodging during the last twelve months.

JOHN: Nonsense, darling. I won't hear of such a thing. I don't want you to pay for your board and lodging.

CONSTANCE: I insist.

JOHN: Don't you love me any more?

CONSTANCE: What has that to do with it? Oh, you think a woman can only love a man if he keeps her. Isn't that rating your powers of fascination too modestly? What about your charm and good humour?

JOHN: Don't be absurd, Constance. I can perfectly well afford to support you in your proper station. To offer me a thousand pounds for your board and lodging is almost insulting.

CONSTANCE: Don't you think it's the kind of insult you could bring yourself to swallow? One can do a lot of amusing things with a thousand pounds.

JOHN: I wouldn't dream of taking it. I never liked the idea of your going into business. I thought you had quite enough to do looking after the house and so forth.

CONSTANCE: Have you been less comfortable since I began working?

JOHN: No, I can't say I have.

CONSTANCE: You can take my word for it, a lot of incompetent women talk a great deal of nonsense about housekeeping. If you know your job and have good servants it can be done in ten minutes a day.

JOHN: Anyhow you wanted to work and I yielded. I thought in point of fact it would be a very pleasant occupation for you, but heavens knows, I wasn't expecting to profit financially by it.

CONSTANCE: No, I'm sure you weren't.

JOHN: Constance, I could never help thinking that your determination had something to do with Marie-Louise.

[*There is a moment's pause and when* CONSTANCE *speaks it is not without seriousness.*]

CONSTANCE: Haven't you wondered why I never reproached you for your affair with Marie-Louise?

JOHN: Yes. I could only ascribe it to your unfathomable goodness.

CONSTANCE: You were wrong. I felt I hadn't the right to reproach you.

JOHN: What do you mean, Constance? You had every right. We behaved like a couple of swine. I may be a dirty dog, but, thank God, I know I'm a dirty dog.

CONSTANCE: You no longer desired me. How could I blame you for that? But if you didn't desire me, what use was I to you? You've seen how small a share I take in providing you with the comfort of a well-ordered home.

JOHN: You were the mother of my child.

CONSTANCE: Let us not exaggerate the importance of that, John. I performed a natural and healthy function of my sex. And all the tiresome part of looking after the child when she was born I placed in the hands of much more competent persons. Let us face it, I was only a parasite in your house. You had entered into legal obligations that prevented you from turning me adrift, but I owe you a debt of gratitude for never letting me see by word or gesture that I was no more than a costly and at times inconvenient ornament.

JOHN: I never looked upon you as an inconvenient ornament. And I don't know what you mean by being a parasite. Have I ever in any way suggested that I grudged a penny that I spent on you?

CONSTANCE [*With mock amazement*]: Do you mean to say that I ascribed to your beautiful manners what was only due to your stupidity? Are you as great a fool as the average man who falls for the average woman's stupendous bluff that just because he's married her he must provide for her wants and her luxuries, sacrifice his pleasures and comfort and convenience, and that he must look upon it as a privilege that she allows him to be her slave and bondman? Come, come, John, pull yourself together. You're a hundred years behind the times. Now that women have broken down the walls of the harem they must take the rough-and-tumble of the street.

JOHN: You forget all sorts of things. Don't you think a man may have gratitude to a woman for the love he has had for her in the past?

CONSTANCE: I think gratitude is often very strong in men so long as it demands from them no particular sacrifices.

JOHN: Well, it's a curious way of looking at things, but obviously I have reason to be thankful for it. But after all you knew what was going on long before it came out. What happened then that made you make up your mind to go into business?

CONSTANCE: I am naturally a lazy woman. So long as appearances were saved I was prepared to take all I could get and give nothing in return. I was a parasite, but I knew

it. But when we reached a situation where only your polite-
ness or your lack of intelligence prevented you from throwing the fact in my teeth I changed my mind. I thought that I
should very much like to be in a position where, if I felt inclined to, I could tell you, with calm, courtesy, but with determination—to go to hell.

JOHN: And are you in that position now?

CONSTANCE: Precisely. I owe you nothing. I am able to
keep myself. For the last year I have paid my way. There is
only one freedom that is really important and that is economic freedom, for in the long run the man who pays the
piper calls the tune. Well, I have that freedom and upon my
soul it's the most enjoyable sensation I can remember since
I ate my first strawberry ice.

JOHN: You know, I would sooner you had made me scenes
for a month on end like any ordinary woman and nagged my
life out than that you should harbour this cold rancour
against me.

CONSTANCE: My poor darling, what are you talking
about? Have you known me for fifteen years and do you
think me capable of the commonness of insincerity? I harbour no rancour. Why, my dear, I'm devoted to you.

JOHN: Do you mean to tell me that you've done all this
without any intention of making me feel a perfect cad?

CONSTANCE: On my honour. If I look in my heart I can
only find in it affection for you and the most kindly and
charitable feelings. Don't you believe me?

[*He looks at her for a moment and then makes a little
gesture of bewilderment.*]

JOHN: Yes, oddly enough, I do. You are a remarkable
woman, Constance.

CONSTANCE: I know, but keep it to yourself. You don't
want to give a dog a bad name.

JOHN [*With an affectionate smile*]: I wish I could get
away. I don't half like the idea of your travelling by yourself.

CONSTANCE: Oh, but I'm not. Didn't I tell you?

JOHN: No.

CONSTANCE: I meant to. I'm going with Bernard.

JOHN: Oh. You never said so. Who else?

CONSTANCE: Nobody.

JOHN: Oh! [*He is rather taken aback at the news*] Isn't that rather odd?

CONSTANCE: No. Why?

JOHN [*Not knowing at all how to take it*]: Well, it's not usual for a young woman to take a six weeks' holiday with a man who can hardly be described as old enough to be her father.

CONSTANCE: Bernard's just about the same age as you.

JOHN: Don't you think it'll make people gossip a bit?

CONSTANCE: I haven't gone out of my way to spread the news. In fact, now I come to think of it, I haven't told any one but you, and you, I am sure, will be discreet.

[JOHN *suddenly feels that his collar is a little too tight for him, and with his fingers he tries to loosen it.*]

JOHN: You're pretty certain to be seen by some one who knows you and they're bound to talk.

CONSTANCE: Oh, I don't think so. You see we're motoring all the way and we neither of us care for frequented places. One of the advantages of having really nice friends like ours is that you can always be certain of finding them at the fashionable resorts at the very moment when everybody you know is there.

JOHN: Of course I am not so silly as to think that because a man and a woman go away together it is necessary to believe the worst about them, but you can't deny that it is rather unconventional. I wouldn't for a moment suggest that there'll be anything between you, but it's inevitable that ordinary persons should think there was.

CONSTANCE [*As cool as a cucumber*]: I've always thought that ordinary persons had more sense than the clever ones are ready to credit them with.

JOHN [*Deliberately*]: What on earth do you mean?

CONSTANCE: Why, of course we're going as man and wife, John.

JOHN: Don't be a fool, Constance. You don't know what you're talking about. That's not funny at all.

CONSTANCE: But, my poor John, whom do you take us for? Am I so unattractive that what I'm telling you is incredible? Why else should I go with Bernard? If I merely wanted a companion I'd go with a woman. We could have headaches together and have our hair washed at the same place and copy one another's nightdresses. A woman's a much better travelling companion than a man.

JOHN: I may be very stupid, but I don't seem to be able to understand what you're saying. Do you really mean me to believe that Bernard Kersal is your lover?

CONSTANCE: Certainly not.

JOHN: Then what *are* you talking about?

CONSTANCE: My dear, I can't put it any plainer. I'm going away for six weeks' holiday and Bernard has very kindly offered to come with me.

JOHN: And where do I come in?

CONSTANCE: You don't come in. You stay at home and look after your patients.

JOHN [*Trying his best to control himself*]: I flatter myself I'm a sensible man. I'm not going to fly into a passion. Many men would stamp and rave or break the furniture. I have no intention of being melodramatic, but you must allow me to say that what you've just told me is very surprising.

CONSTANCE: Just for a moment, perhaps, but I'm sure you have only to familiarize yourself with the notion in order to become reconciled to it.

JOHN: I'm doubtful whether I shall have time to do that, for I feel uncommonly as though I were about to have an apoplectic stroke.

CONSTANCE: Undo your collar then. Now I come to look at you I confess that you are more than usually red in the face.

JOHN: What makes you think that I am going to allow you to go?

CONSTANCE [*Good-humouredly*]: Chiefly the fact that you can't prevent me.

JOHN: I can't bring myself to believe that you mean what you say. I don't know what ever put such an idea into your head.

CONSTANCE [*Casually*]: I thought a change might do me good.

JOHN: Nonsense.

CONSTANCE: Why? You did. Don't you remember? You were getting rather flat and stale. Then you had an affair with Marie-Louise and you were quite another man. Gay and amusing, full of life, and much more agreeable to live with. The moral effect on you was quite remarkable.

JOHN: It's different for a man than for a woman.

CONSTANCE: Are you thinking of the possible consequences? We have long passed the Victorian Era when asterisks were followed after a certain interval by a baby.

JOHN: That never occurred to me. What I meant was that if a man's unfaithful to his wife she's an object of sympathy, whereas if a woman's unfaithful to her husband he's merely an object of ridicule.

CONSTANCE: That is one of those conventional prejudices that sensible people must strive to ignore.

JOHN: Do you expect me to sit still and let this man take my wife away from under my very nose? I wonder you don't ask me to shake hands with him and wish him good luck.

CONSTANCE: That's just what I am going to do. He's coming here in a few minutes to say good-bye to you.

JOHN: I shall knock him down.

CONSTANCE: I wouldn't take any risks in your place. He's pretty hefty and I'm under the impression that he's very nippy with his left.

JOHN: I shall have great pleasure in telling him exactly what I think of him.

CONSTANCE: Why? Have you forgotten that I am charming to Marie-Louise? We were the best of friends. She never bought a hat without asking me to go and help her choose it.

JOHN: I have red blood in my veins.

CONSTANCE: I'm more concerned at the moment with the grey matter in your brain.

JOHN: Is he in love with you?

CONSTANCE: Madly. Didn't you know?

JOHN: I? How should I?

CONSTANCE: He's been here a great deal during the last year. Were you under the impression that he only came to see you?

JOHN: I never paid any attention to him. I thought him rather dull.

CONSTANCE: He is rather dull. But he's very sweet.

JOHN: What sort of a man is it who eats a fellow's food and drinks his wine and then makes love to his wife behind his back?

CONSTANCE: A man very like you, John, I should say.

JOHN: Not at all. Mortimer is the sort of man who was born to be made a fool of.

CONSTANCE: None of us know for certain the designs of providence.

JOHN: I see you're bent on driving me to desperation. I shall break something in a minute.

CONSTANCE: There's that blue-and-white bowl that your Uncle Henry gave us as a wedding present. Break that, it's only a modern imitation.

[*He takes the bowl and hurls it on the floor so that it is shattered.*]

JOHN: There.

CONSTANCE: Do you feel better?

JOHN: Not a bit.

CONSTANCE: It's a pity you broke it then. You might have given it away as a wedding present to one of your colleagues at the hospital.

[*The butler shows in* MRS. CULVER.]

BUTLER: Mrs. Culver.

CONSTANCE: Oh, mother, how sweet of you to come. I was so hoping I'd see you before I left.

MRS. CULVER: Oh, you've had an accident.

CONSTANCE: No, John's in a temper and he thought it would relieve him if he broke something.

MRS. CULVER: Nonsense, John's never in a temper.

JOHN: That's what you think, Mrs. Culver. Yes, I am in a temper. I'm in a filthy temper. Are you a party to this plan of Constance's?

CONSTANCE: No, mother doesn't know.

JOHN: Can't you do something to stop it? You have some influence over her. You must see that the thing's preposterous.

John: If you think what they call free love is fun you're vastly mistaken. Believe me, it's the most overrated amusement that was ever invented. I know.

MRS. CULVER: My dear boy, I haven't the ghost of an idea what you're talking about.

JOHN: She's going to Italy with Bernard Kersal. Alone.

MRS. CULVER [*With a stare*]: It's not true; how d'you know?

JOHN: She's just told me so, as bold as brass, out of a blue sky. She mentioned it in the course of conversation as if she were saying: "Darling, your coat wants brushing."

MRS. CULVER: Is it true, Constance?

CONSTANCE: Quite.

MRS. CULVER: But haven't you been getting on with John? I always thought you two were as happy as the day is long.

JOHN: So did I. We've never had the shadow of a quarrel. We've always got on.

MRS. CULVER: Don't you love John any more, darling?

CONSTANCE: Yes, I'm devoted to him.

JOHN: How can you be devoted to a man when you're going to do him the greatest injury that a woman can do to a man?

CONSTANCE: Don't be idiotic, John. I'm going to do you no more injury than you did me a year ago.

JOHN [*Striding up to her, thinking quite erroneously that he sees light*]: Are you doing this in order to pay me out for Marie-Louise?

CONSTANCE: Don't be such a fool, John. Nothing is further from my thoughts.

MRS. CULVER: The circumstances are entirely different. It was very naughty of John to deceive you, but he's sorry for what he did and he's been punished for it. It was all very dreadful and caused us a great deal of pain. But a man's a man and you expect that kind of thing from him. There are excuses for him. There are none for a woman. Men are naturally polygamous and sensible women have always made allowances for their occasional lapse from a condition which modern civilisation has forced on them. Women are monogamous. They do not naturally desire more than one man and that is why the common sense of the world has heaped obloquy upon them when they have overstepped the natural limitations of their sex.

CONSTANCE [*Smiling*]: It seems rather hard that what is sauce for the gander shouldn't also be sauce for the goose.

MRS. CULVER: We all know that unchastity has no moral effect on men. They can be perfectly promiscuous and remain upright, industrious and reliable. It's quite different with women. It ruins their character. They become untruthful and dissipated, lazy, shiftless and dishonest. That is why the experience of ten thousand years has demanded chastity in women. Because it has learnt that this virtue is the key to all others.

CONSTANCE: They were dishonest because they were giving away something that wasn't theirs to give. They had sold themselves for board, lodging and protection. They were chattel. They were dependent on their husbands and when they were unfaithful to them they were liars and thieves. I'm not dependent on John. I am economically independent and therefore I claim my sexual independence. I have this afternoon paid into John's account one thousand pounds for my year's keep.

JOHN: I refuse to take it.

CONSTANCE: Well, you'll damned well have to.

MRS. CULVER: There's no object in losing your temper.

CONSTANCE: I have mine under perfect control.

JOHN: If you think what they call free love is fun, you're mistaken. Believe me, it's the most overrated amusement that was ever invented.

CONSTANCE: In that case, I wonder why people continue to indulge in it.

JOHN: I ought to know what I'm talking about, hang it all. It has all the inconveniences of marriage and none of its advantages. I assure you, my dear, the game is not worth the candle.

CONSTANCE: You may be right, but you know how hard it is to profit by anybody's experience. I think I'd like to see for myself.

MRS. CULVER: Are you in love with Bernard?

CONSTANCE: To tell you the truth I haven't quite made up my mind. How does one know if one's in love?

MRS. CULVER: My dear, I only know one test. Could you use his tooth-brush?

CONSTANCE: No.

MRS. CULVER: Then you're not in love with him.

CONSTANCE: He's adored me for fifteen years. There's something in that long devotion which gives me a funny little feeling in my heart. I should like to do something to show him that I'm not ungrateful. You see, in six weeks he goes back to Japan. There is no chance of his coming to England again for seven years. I'm thirty-six now and he adores me; in seven years I shall be forty-three. A woman of forty-three is often charming, but it's seldom that a man of fifty-five is crazy about her. I came to the conclusion that it must be now or never and so I asked him if he'd like me to spend these last six weeks with him in Italy. When I wave my handkerchief to him as the ship that takes him sails out of the harbour at Naples I hope that he will feel that all those years of unselfish love have been well worth the while.

JOHN: Six weeks. Do you intend to leave him at the end of six weeks?

CONSTANCE: Oh, yes, of course. It's because I'm putting a limit to our love that I think it may achieve the perfection of something that is beautiful and transitory. Why, John, what is it that makes a rose so lovely but that its petals fall as soon as it is full blown?

JOHN: It's all come as such a shock and a surprise that I hardly know what to say. You've got me at a complete disadvantage.

[MRS. CULVER, *who has been standing at the window, gives a little cry.*]

CONSTANCE: What is it?

MRS. CULVER: Here is Bernard. He's just driven up to the door.

JOHN: Do you expect me to receive him as if I were blissfully unconscious of your plans?

CONSTANCE: It would be more comfortable. It would be stupid to make a scene and it wouldn't prevent my going on this little jaunt with him.

JOHN: I have my dignity to think of.

CONSTANCE: One often preserves that best by putting it in one's pocket. It would be kind of you, John, to treat him just as pleasantly as I treated Marie-Louise when I knew she was your mistress.

JOHN: Does he know that I know?

CONSTANCE: Of course not. He's a little conventional, you know, and he couldn't happily deceive a friend if he thought there was no deception.

MRS. CULVER: Constance, is there nothing I can say to make you reconsider your decision?

CONSTANCE: Nothing, darling.

MRS. CULVER: Then I may just as well save my breath. I'll slip away before he comes.

CONSTANCE: Oh, all right. Good-bye, mother. I'll send you a lot of picture post-cards.

MRS. CULVER: I don't approve of you, Constance, and I can't pretend that I do. No good will come of it. Men were meant by nature to be wicked and delightful and deceive their wives, and women were meant to be virtuous and for-giving and to suffer verbosely. That was ordained from all eternity and none of your new-fangled notions can alter the decrees of Providence.

[*The butler enters, followed by* BERNARD.]

BENTLEY: Mr. Kersal.

MRS. CULVER: How do you do, Bernard, and good-bye. I'm just going.

BERNARD: Oh, I'm sorry. Good-bye.

[*She goes out.*]

CONSTANCE [*To* BERNARD]: How d'you do. Just one mo-ment. [*To the butler*] Oh, Bentley, get my things downstairs and put them in a taxi, will you?

BENTLEY: Very good, madam.

BERNARD: Are you just starting? It's lucky I came when I did. I should have hated to miss you.

CONSTANCE: And let me know when the taxi's here.

BENTLEY: Yes, madam.

CONSTANCE: Now I can attend to you. [*The butler goes out.*]

BERNARD: Are you looking forward to your holiday?

CONSTANCE: Immensely. I've never gone on a jaunt like this before, and I'm really quite excited.

BERNARD: You're going alone, aren't you?

CONSTANCE: Oh, yes, quite alone.

BERNARD: It's rotten for you not to be able to get away, old man.

JOHN: Rotten.

BERNARD: I suppose these are the penalties of greatness. I can quite understand that you have to think of your patients first.

JOHN: Quite.

CONSTANCE: Of course John doesn't very much care for Italy.

BERNARD: Oh, are you going to Italy? I thought you said Spain.

JOHN: No, she always said Italy.

BERNARD: Oh, well, that's hardly your mark, is it, old boy? Though I believe there are some sporting links on the Lake of Como.

JOHN: Are there?

BERNARD: I suppose there's no chance of your being anywhere near Naples towards the end of July?

CONSTANCE: I don't really know. My plans are quite vague.

BERNARD: I was only asking because I'm sailing from Naples. It would be fun if we met there.

JOHN: Great fun.

CONSTANCE: I hope you'll see a lot of John while I'm away. I'm afraid he'll be a trifle lonely, poor darling. Why don't you dine together one day next week?

BERNARD: I'm terribly sorry, but you know I'm going away.

CONSTANCE: Oh, are you? I thought you were going to stay in London till you had to start for Japan.

BERNARD: I meant to, but my doctor has ordered me to go and do a cure.

JOHN: What sort of a cure?

BERNARD: Oh, just a cure. He says I want bucking up.

JOHN: Oh, does he? What's the name of your doctor?

BERNARD: No one you ever heard of. A man I used to know in the war.

JOHN: Oh!

BERNARD: So I'm afraid this is good-bye. Of course, it's a wrench leaving London, especially as I don't expect to be in Europe again for some years, but I always think it rather silly not to take a man's advice when you've asked for it.

JOHN: More especially when he's charged you three guineas.

CONSTANCE: I'm sorry. I was counting on you to keep John out of mischief during my absence.

BERNARD: I'm not sure if I could guarantee to do that. But we might have done a few theatres together and had a game of golf or two.

CONSTANCE: It would have been jolly, wouldn't it, John?

JOHN: Very jolly.

[*The butler comes in.*]

BENTLEY: The taxi's waiting, madam.

CONSTANCE: Thank you.

[*The butler goes out.*]

BERNARD: I'll take myself off. In case I don't see you again I'd like to thank you now for all your kindness to me during the year I've spent in London.

CONSTANCE: It's been very nice to see you.

BERNARD: You and John have been most awfully good to me. I never imagined I was going to have such a wonderful time.

CONSTANCE: We shall miss you terribly. It's been a great comfort to John to think that there was some one to take me out when he had to be away on one of his operations. Hasn't it, darling?

JOHN: Yes, darling.

CONSTANCE: When he knew I was with you he never worried. Did you, darling?

JOHN: No, darling.

BERNARD: I'm awfully glad if I've been able to make myself useful. Don't forget me entirely, will you?

CONSTANCE: We're not likely to do that, are we, darling?

JOHN: No, darling.

BERNARD: And if you ever have a moment to spare you will write to me, won't you? You don't know how much it means to us exiles.

CONSTANCE: Of course we will. We'll both write. Won't we, darling?

JOHN: Yes, darling.

CONSTANCE: John writes such a good letter. So chatty, you know, and amusing.

BERNARD: That's a promise. Well, good-bye, old boy. Have a good time.

JOHN: Thanks, old bean.

BERNARD: Good-bye, Constance. There's so much I want to say to you that I don't know where to begin.

JOHN: I don't want to hurry you, but the taxi is just ticking its head off.

BERNARD: John is so matter-of-fact. Well, I'll say nothing then but God bless you.

CONSTANCE: Au revoir.

BERNARD: If you do go to Naples you will let me know, won't you? If you send a line to my club, it'll be forwarded at once.

CONSTANCE: Oh, all right.

BERNARD: Good-bye.

   [*He gives them both a friendly nod and goes out.* CONSTANCE *begins to giggle and soon is seized with uncontrollable laughter.*]

JOHN: Will you kindly tell what there is to laugh at? If you think it amuses me to stand here like patience on a monument and have my leg pulled you're mistaken. What did you mean by all that balderdash about meeting you by chance in Naples?

CONSTANCE: He was throwing you off the scent.

JOHN: The man's a drivelling idiot.

CONSTANCE: D'you think so? I thought he was rather ingenious. Considering he hasn't had very much practice in this sort of thing I thought he did very well.

JOHN: Of course if you're determined to find him a pattern of perfection it's useless for me to attempt to argue. But honestly, speaking without prejudice for or against, I'm sorry to think of you throwing yourself away on a man like that.

CONSTANCE: Perhaps it's natural that a man and his wife should differ in their estimate of her prospective lover.

JOHN: You're not going to tell me he's better-looking than I am.

CONSTANCE: No. You have always been my ideal of manly beauty.

JOHN: He's no better dressed than I am.

CONSTANCE: He could hardly expect to be. He goes to the same tailor.

JOHN: I don't think you can honestly say he's more amusing than I am.

CONSTANCE: No, I honestly can't.

JOHN: Then in Heaven's name why do you want to go away with him?

CONSTANCE: Shall I tell you? Once more before it's too late I want to feel about me the arms of a man who adores the ground I walk on. I want to see his face light up when I enter the room. I want to feel the pressure of his hand when we look at the moon together and the pleasantly tickling sensation when his arm tremulously steals around my waist. I want to let my hand fall on his shoulder and feel his lips softly touch my hair.

JOHN: The operation is automatically impossible, the poor devil would get such a crick in the neck he wouldn't know what to do.

CONSTANCE: I want to walk along country lanes holding hands and I want to be called by absurd pet names. I want to talk baby-talk by the hour together.

JOHN: Oh, God.

CONSTANCE: I want to know that I'm eloquent and witty when I'm dead silent. For ten years I've been very happy in your affections, John, we've been the best and dearest friends, but now just for a little while I hanker for something else. Do you grudge it me? I want to be loved.

JOHN: But, my dear, I'll love you. I've been a brute, I've neglected you, it's not too late and you're the only woman I've ever really cared for. I'll chuck everything and we'll go away together.

CONSTANCE: The prospect does not thrill me.

JOHN: Come, darling, have a heart. I gave up Marie-Louise. Surely you can give up Bernard.

CONSTANCE: But you gave up Marie-Louise to please yourself, not to please me.

JOHN: Don't be a little beast, Constance. Come away with me. We'll have such a lark.

CONSTANCE: Oh, my poor John, I didn't work so hard to gain my economic independence in order to go on a honeymoon with my own husband.

JOHN: Do you think I can't be a lover as well as a husband?

CONSTANCE: My dear, no one can make yesterday's cold mutton into to-morrow's lamb cutlets.

JOHN: You know what you're doing. I was determined in future to be a model husband and you're driving me right into the arms of Marie-Louise. I give you my word of honour that the moment you leave this house I shall drive straight to her door.

CONSTANCE: I should hate you to have a fruitless journey. I'm afraid you won't find her at home. She has a new young man and she says he's too divine.

JOHN: What!

CONSTANCE: He's the A.D.C. of a Colonial Governor. She came here to-day to ask me to break the news to you that henceforth everything was over between you.

JOHN: I hope you told her first that I was firmly resolved to terminate a connection that could only cause you pain.

CONSTANCE: I couldn't. She was in such a blooming hurry to give me her message.

JOHN: Really, Constance, for your own pride I should have thought you wouldn't like her to make a perfect fool of me. Any other woman would have said: "What a strange coincidence. Why it's only half an hour since John told me he had made up his mind never to see you again." But of course you don't care two straws for me any more, that's quite evident.

CONSTANCE: Oh, don't be unjust, darling. I shall always care for you. I may be unfaithful, but I am constant. I always think that's my most endearing quality.

[*The butler opens the door.*]

JOHN [*Irritably*]: What is it?

BENTLEY: I thought madam had forgotten that the taxi was at the door.

JOHN: Go to hell.

BENTLEY: Very good, sir.

[*He goes out.*]

CONSTANCE: I don't see why you should be rude to him. Bernard will pay the taxi. Anyhow I must go now or he'll begin to think I'm not coming. Good-bye, darling. I hope you'll get on all right in my absence. Just give the cook her head and you'll have no trouble. Won't you say good-bye to me?

JOHN: Go to the devil.

CONSTANCE: All right. I shall be back in six weeks.

JOHN: Back? Where?

CONSTANCE: Here.

JOHN: Here? Here? Do you think I'm going to take you back?

CONSTANCE: I don't see why not. When you've had time to reflect you'll realise that you have no reason to blame me. After all, I'm taking from you nothing that you want.

JOHN: Are you aware that I can divorce you for this?

CONSTANCE: Quite. But I married very prudently. I took the precaution to marry a gentleman and I know that you could never bring yourself to divorce me for doing no more than you did yourself.

JOHN: I wouldn't divorce you. I wouldn't expose my worst enemy to the risk of marrying a woman who's capable of treating her husband as you're treating me.

CONSTANCE [*At the door*]: Well, then, shall I come back?

JOHN [*After a moment's hesitation*]: You are the most maddening, wilful, capricious, wrong-headed, delightful and enchanting woman man was ever cursed with having for a wife. Yes, damn you, come back.

[*She lightly kisses her hand to him and slips out, slamming the door behind her.*]

THE END